$\mathcal{S}$EEDS OF...

VOLUME II

To Sharon
Isaiah 40:31 —
Mason R Brown
(Karen R Brown)

A TAWK PRESS ANTHOLOGY
OF PACIFIC NW WRITERS

what fruits of tomorrow
but grow from
seeds of
yesterday —
or today?
mjN

"Don't judge each day by the harvest you reap,
but by the seeds you plant."
Robert Louis Stevenson

$\mathcal{S}$EEDS OF...

VOLUME II

A TAWK Press Anthology
of Pacific NW Writers

Edited by Mary Jane Nordgren

Graphic Art by Wm. A. Helwig

ISBN   978-0970389640

Additional copies of this book are available at CreatSpace.com

PUBLISHED by
TAWK Press, 47777 S.W. Ihrig Road, Forest Grove, OR 97116

*This book is dedicated to Writers in the Grove and so many support-
ive friends, writers and not-yet-writers - mj*

TABLE OF CONTENTS
Seeds of...   Volume II

SECTION I – COPING

SECTION II – RELATING

SECTION III - FINDING SELF

SECTION IV – REMEMBERING

SECTION V – REFLECTING

Seeds of...

Section I – Coping

Kissinger

(Excerpt from Dante's Angels)

By D. K. Lubarsky

Helen arrived late; disheveled, red lipstick smudged on her front teeth, dark brown hair uncombed, mismatched shoes. She pulled out a chair, plopped her purse on the floor and looked at her friends.

"None of you will ever love me again," she moaned. "I'm a murderer!"

Four pair of eyes stared at her.

"What?"

"I killed Kissinger."

Thirty seconds of silence followed.

Bella spoke first. "Honey, Henry Kissinger died a long time ago."

"Really?" whispered Ruth. "I thought he was still alive."

"It doesn't matter whether he's dead or alive. He's old," added Estelle.

"Well, if he died a long time ago Helen couldn't have killed him. And if he's alive I guess she didn't do a very good job." Ginger looked Helen directly in the eye. "Either way you're in the clear, so why don't you just tell us what happened while I look up Kissinger on Google. We'll find out in a minute if he is dead or alive." She rummaged through her purse, found her IPhone and began punching buttons. "My daughter showed me how to work this damn thing yesterday. If I can only remember ..."

"It wasn't HENRY Kissinger!" Helen wailed. "It was "Tweety-bird Kissinger."

Ginger put down her IPhone.

Estelle fumbled with the volume switch on her hearing aid.

"My canary!" Helen shrieked. "I vacuumed him. It was an accident! I swear!"

"Now let me get this straight. You have a canary named Kissinger..." Ruth said coughing up her last bite of scrambled eggs.

"Had," interrupted Helen. "He died."

"In the vacuum cleaner?"

"Yes."

Ruth, Estelle, Ginger and Bella stared at Helen for a few seconds before their chuckles turned into roaring laughter.

"It's not funny!" Helen cried, bouncing between tears and giggles. "He was a good little bird!"

"This I've got to hear." Ruth blew her nose, stuffed the used tissue into the cuff of her left sleeve and leaned back in her chair.

"Well, my two sons, their wives, and six grandkids were coming over to our house for dinner last night. I worked all day cleaning and cooking and by five o'clock I was exhausted. Meanwhile, the stew was burning, the phone kept ringing, I cut my finger slicing the salad, and then I tripped over the damn vacuum cleaner. That's when Kissinger got loose. He flew up to the cornice in the living room and wouldn't come down.

He's usually so good when I call. But not last night. I called and called, but he wouldn't come. I felt myself getting angrier and angrier at that damn bird. And that's when it happened."

"What happened?" they shouted in unison.

"Kissinger flew down off the cornice, circled around me once and shit on my head. I was so furious that I just grabbed that damn vacuum cleaner, aimed … and the next thing I heard was this loud 'THWAT' sound … and Kissinger was gone."

"You vacuumed Kissinger?"

"Yes. I did. Stupid bird. It took a few seconds before I realized what I'd done. I ran to the vacuum, ripped the canister open and there lay Kissinger, on his back, with his feet curled up under him, dead as a doornail. And of course just at that very second the front door burst open and all the grandkids charged into the living room yelling 'Hi Grammy!' Lucy and Emma and all the rest of them took one look at Kissinger, dead in the vacuum cleaner, and they ran out of the room screaming their heads off. It took more than a half hour to calm them all down. I felt just awful. I tried to act nonchalant for the sake of the children, but my heart was racing and I thought I was going to throw up. Thank God, Bill came to the rescue. He picked up Kissinger and put him in the garage so we could bury him after they all left."

"Oh honey," said Ginger, "losing a pet is hard anytime, but that's taking it to a whole new level."

"Oh, it got much worse after that. Halfway through dinner Keith announced that he and Lindsay were getting a divorce, he was gay, and this fellow he's been hanging out with lately is his new partner. If I didn't pass out at that moment I swear I never will." She sighed. "And quite frankly that's all I remember about the entire evening."

"Wow," murmured the group.

"I mean, we knew something was wrong with their marriage," Helen continued, "Lindsay has been so difficult these last two years. We never guessed why. His announcement last night really rocked our foundation. It's going to take a while to process. Made me wonder if I really know anything about anyone. Even my own son."

They all nodded, thoughts turning inward to their own families.

"Kids. You conceive them, grow them, give birth to them and raise them with all the love you possess. You change your world so that it revolves around them. You do everything for them. They become your center. And then one day you look up and they are gone, and in their place are these grown people. They look like your own children, but their lives are a mystery to you. They have secrets, lots of secrets, and you realize you know nothing at all about these strangers standing in front of you. How does that happen?"

"Did you ever suspect?" Ginger whispered.

"If I can be dirt honest, I think I might have. But it was just one of those thoughts that flit through your mind, and then you let it go and think, nah, couldn't be. After all he has a wife and two kids."

"How's Bill taking it?" asked Ruth.

"Not well. He looked like a bomb went off inside him, but he didn't say a word. When Bill gets upset he just turns his feelings in and grits his teeth. After everyone left he buried Kissinger in the back yard and then went straight to bed. Refused to talk to me. Same thing this morning."

"It's going to be all right," said Estelle. "There's a couple of ladies living three doors down from me. They are so warm and friendly. It's not how it used to be, you know. Now-a- days it is okay to be gay. And you still have all the grandkids. So you've got the best of both worlds. And if you need any more inspiration just think of Maureen O'Hara."

"Maureen O'Hara?"

"Anderson Cooper's mother. I mean, he's so cute, and she must be so proud of him."

Ruth's eyebrows knit together. "I think you mean Gloria Vanderbilt."

"Vanderbilt, O'Hara, what's the difference? He's adorable. I watch him every night on the television." Estelle smiled and reached out to take Helen's hand. "You, Bill and Keith will be just fine."

"Thanks, sweetie," Helen smiled sorrowfully.

Just then Roger swung by. "Well ladies, are you all ready to order yet?" he called on his way into the kitchen.

"Yes," said Ginger after a long silence. "But first, we need to make a toast to Kissinger!"

"To Kissinger!" the group yelled, energetically raising their water tumblers overhead.

The sound of breaking glass permeated the dinner as all five glasses collided in the center of the table. Roger took one look, dropped his pad and pencil and went running for the mop.

Clair's Quiet Corner

By Ross Hall

Mental health people are such a strange lot. I could never do what they do, and I dislike seeing them. But they have helped me to achieve focus. Charley is dead, his body burnt to a crisp in Afghanistan. All that jabber about the number of stages of grief didn't really connect except to let me know that there are stages and that I have no choice but to go through them.

Or to die, and even that is not easy.

My stages were "zombie one" (without booze), "zombie two" (with booze), to admitting his death and that unholy vacuum, to "screw them all," to "screw it all," and finally to finding meaning in the mundane.

Each of my stages had taken a different length of time to work. Both of the "zombie" stages were too long and the second one nearly killed me. But the last stage, which is still going on, may go on forever.

First it was clean dishes and then clean house.

Next I learned to knit sweaters, which forced me to give them away. So that led to finding worthy beneficiaries of my prolific and middling skills. Which, in turn, ended my life as a recluse, leading me back to people. Many of the ones who had seemed to have benign resignation of this war and to accept the deceit and manipulation that led to Charlie's brutal death. I imagined them cheering on that war nonsense. They are now, of course, immense friends, outspoken about our evil conniving government, and who are helping in the healing. But when I saw one of the sweaters at a garage sale, I admitted that it was time to learn new artistic outlets.

My first new creative endeavor allowed them, the seemingly unobtrusive natural multitude, to get control of me. It was moving to David's house with the half acre out back that began the trickery. I know now that they seduced me. The first year I was reluctant and my efforts were restrained.

The second year I was willing and earnest but didn't really understand their elemental strategy. But last year and again this year I have been most enthusiastic and now willingly do the bidding of these plants. The corn, beans, peas, squash and tomatoes are my masters in the growing season. I love preparing their beds, working the soil to get healthy mulch around the seedlings, and I am filled with anticipation watching them grow and offer their harvest to me. They may think that I believe that I am the controlling consciousness here, that I might think I am in control because I place the seeds and give them water and improve their surroundings. But they have tricked me into doing what is necessary for them to multiply. And I will! As I have struck the bargain. They need me and I desire them. Their tasty constraints hold me. So I let each one know.

"Well, Seed Corn, I want you to know that I selected you especially. You will grow tall and give me sweet ears. You will be beautiful stalks of grass with silken wisps of gold on your fruit. I believe you to be the most magnificent grass ever grown, occupying an elegant domain. Garrison Keillor tells me on the radio that eating fresh corn on the cob is better than sex. And I know what he says to be true, though there is a certain David to whom I will not mention that fact. So you and your colleagues flourish here. And I will be bringing you water, praying for sunshine."

I also speak to the nasturtiums, the sunflowers, and the other flowering flora, explaining to them their role in this sanctuary.

They are to provide a welcome to growing things, including the birds, the squirrels, raccoon's, bees, and other courteous visitors. With David's help I have built a blowsy, but beautiful berm around the garden, covered with bursts of color, defining the periphery of this revered region.

I feel an obligation to make observations with a modicum of profundity about this botanical bargain, my horticultural hex. Something about lost life, pain, recovery, and renewal.

But, all I can say is that during that special two weeks I noticed that the zucchini grew eighteen inches; that David loved to walk through my garden issuing enthusiastic compliments; that the snap peas were a big hit at the September birthday dinner. My smile returns daily now. I am willingly under the spell of the growing life in that cloistered half-acre behind the house. I am spreading the mulch now and can hardly wait until Spring.

The Squirrels Speak To Me

By Joe Schrader

I don't need to get my news
From those fellows on TV;
I don't need to read the paper,
'Cuz the squirrels speak to me.

They hand me down the Word of God
From that pulpit in their tree;
I get scripture and salvation
When those squirrels speak to me.

My family surely think I'm nuts,
They so righteously determine
I need treatment psychiatric
When I repeat those squirrelly sermons.

It started just three years ago,
While on my daily walk;
I'd stopped to watch the sunrise,
When I heard their chattered talk.

At first it was just pleasantries,
And bits of local news;
Eventually, science and politics,
And philosophic views.

They'd debate on global warming,
And the balance of world trade;
They'd lecture quantum physics,
And the ills of foreign aid.

Yes, I'd really grown enlightened
By those lectures in my yard;
And to grasp their dissertations
It often was quite hard.

Well, I tried to tell the doctors,
But it became quite clear
They'd never fully understand
Those voices that I hear.

They tried many medications,
And that silly Rorschach test;
They even tried shock-therapy,
And asked was I depressed?

So they've put me in this "rest-home",
With a gate that's locked at night;
I've even got a private room...
With windows bolted tight.

But in the day-time, I can stroll
Through gardens with tall trees;
And when the nurses aren't around,
The squirrels still speak to me!

My Very First Christmas

By Lois Akerson

We had celebrated our daughter's 35th birthday in February and in July we gathered for her funeral. Tears and grief consumed me and it was hard to look forward to December and to imagine our traditional family Christmas celebration. I wondered how I could do the things that people usually do at Christmas time. I prayed and asked God to somehow lighten the sorrow that weighted down my heart.

"That's a good idea, Lord," I thought. "I'll see Christmas through the eyes of my little grandson."

Ooh, I'm excited! I see lights! I hear Christmas music! I see lots of faces and they're all smiling at me. I'm David. I'm five and a half months old and this is my very first Christmas. My Daddy has his arm around Mommy. He works hard every day just to buy my applesauce, my formula and my clothes. I guess he buys a few things for Mommy too. Daddy plays fun games with me and makes me giggle.

Mommy is always hugging and kissing me, but I guess that's what Mommies are supposed to do.

Aunty Paula isn't here. Oh, that's right, she's working in Papua New Guinea as a translator. She helped Mommy take care of me when I was born. I remember her singing to me, rocking and changing me.

There's Aunt Debbie with that black camcorder. I wonder if that's her real face?

Oh well, they say there's one in every family. When I get bigger, I hope she'll let me play with her two Bassett hounds, Daffodil and Rusty.

"Hi, David! How's it goin'? Want a piggyback ride?" teases my uncle Eric. Like me, Eric has had some changes this past year too. His night school classes in accounting helped him get a new job with Intel Corporation. He and Aunt Debbie work for the same company and ride to work together.

I miss Aunt Carol and everyone else says they do too. I only saw her a few times before she passed away so I really didn't get to know her very well. But everyone says she was a wonderful person and that she's up in heaven with Jesus now.

"David, what's this?" coos grandma Lois.

Grandma is handing me a present. She's looking at me. What am I supposed to do? I think I'll try to chew it. Ooh, that doesn't taste good at all! I think I'll cry. Grandma just loves to console me. I wish she would quit her job so she could spend more time playing with me.

Boy, it sure got quiet all of a sudden. Oh, I know why. It's 'cause Grandpa Ed is reading the Christmas story. Ssh! Here comes the best part of the story, the part where baby Jesus was born.

I can hardly stay awake. Uh oh, Mommy has noticed me rubbing my eyes. I think I'll have to go to sleep now. Oh well, I guess I can't expect to stay up late at my age. But it sure was fun while it lasted! I think Christmas is a good idea. But, of course, I can't speak from experience, since this is my very first Christmas.

Morning Star

By D. K. Lubarsky

Sweet child of mine with your funny little gait
Head down in forward thrust
Arms flapping at odd angles behind

Sweet child of my child
Running, forward, sideways, zig-zag down the street
So fast I cannot catch you
Laughing

Sweet child of life
Each time you stumble
My heart cries

Have you noticed yet
    that you are different from other children?
I think not.
I hope you never do.

THREE-SIXTY

By Mark Thalman

Pavement a dull sheen
from an early evening shower,
I've got the radio turned up—
singing harmony on Good Vibrations,
when a car pulls out and stops
broadside in my lane.

I stomp the brake, jerk the wheel—
My Chevy Biscayne hydroplanes,
spinning as if on an axis,
a miniature planet.

Twisting the wheel back, I continue
in a straight line, bracing myself—
ready to crash into the man staring at me
like he's just seen a marvelous circus trick.

In the last thousandth of a second,
he gives it gas, and moving out of the way
in the flash of a matador's cape,
the road opens miraculously,
a river of painted stripes,
while dashboard lights glow
low as votive candles,
and the engine hums like a choir.

I come up slow on a red light,
and no longer know my hands
trembling drunk on adrenaline.

It all floods back, the surge
of helplessness,
waiting for impact,
crush of metal, splintering glass—
once again, I am living
the illusion of being safe,
while this planet whirls through space,
me holding tight to the wheel,
steering as if convinced
I have control of my life.

Published in The McGuffin, Fall 2013

slots

By Mary Jane Nordgren

arizona's compressed red sandstone
frazzles into sandpaper wind
but welcomes not a gush of rain
does not absorb its needed
cool moisture, but sheds it
into runoff that gathers with
other rejected trickle, then stream
running headlong across the desert floor
diving, gouging, carving slot canyons
glorious in their smooth, sinuous
twists and bands of color
deep by twice or thrice the height of men
but narrow enough often for man to reach both sides
with outstretched arms
adventurers, unaware they are gambling,
lower themselves into these
slot canyons, awed into silence or quiet comment
explore under fierce blue sky
not knowing storm clouds a score of miles afar
have contributed to a gushing flood
now racing toward the low point
scoured years before along unyielding path

Dear Dorothy,

I hope this letter finds you feeling better.
I understand – Toto 1 and 2 and 3
buried with their bones; all newer Wizards
equally shriveled. I too have waltzed
with Wicked Witches, and yes, they all lack
the chit-chat knack. By the way, thanks
for the lowdown on that spritzing trick.

But unlike yours, *our* roads have never been yellow.
They're either black or white; hard as concrete
or reeky as asphalt. And the scarecrows *we* endure
believe in their brains. *Our* tin men snigger
at hearts, and *our* cowards strut their words
from inside the pride of numbers, *depend* on monsters –
as pastors need devils to gather the ruck,
as tyrants keep order with rumors of racks,
as dogs need cats to tighten the pack.

It is the way of the world:
Some crave monsters, some crave saints.
Tell me which is pumping the people's blood
and I can say if the moon will be red this month.
But this side the page, virtue can't return –
has no home to recover.
We who ponder have only our saints
and the desperate need to follow,
follow as they dim in the fog,
slowly pulling away from us.

By Fred Melden

Loose Ends

By Phil Pochurek

The irony in life is
That it's not the knots
In our lives that hold us back
It's the loose ends.
The unfinished business
The unspoken word,
That's where the trouble begins.
From things left undone or broken
Not said or never heard.
It's an open sore that never heals
Deep inside of us.
The ones no one sees.
But you can feel…
Still raw beneath the layers of years.
Just under the skin
Where the pain is real
Hidden in the quiet moments

But with every new beginning
Comes a new piece of rope.
A life line strong and unfrayed
A tie that binds us to this world with
Something to hold onto when things get tough
So we won't become fearful or afraid.

Don't wait till you're
At the end of your rope
Looking for a knot to hold onto
To keep you afloat
And it's too late to make amends.
When you reach for that knot
To save yourself but all you come up with
Are loose ends.

The Phoenix Legacy

By Bunny Lynne Hansen

In the spring of 1995, Cascade City, Oregon did not look like a war zone. None of its leading citizens would have predicted that such carnage could take place within its borders. It considered itself a refuge, an escape, from civilization's contamination, seated as it was on the shores of a pristine, sapphire lake, surrounded by old growth forests and snow-capped mountains. Locals boasted that it was "God's country." But the native people, the first inhabitants of the land knew different things. They knew it was the battlefield in a war between opposing spirits of two raging volcanoes, Mount Mazama and Mount Shasta. Eons later, modern geologists scientifically confirmed the ancient legends in different language.

New battles in that ancient war broke out in 1995 when a worldwide timetable of death and violence erupted in the sleepy hamlet. That was the year when another mountain village, Srebrenica, Bosnia, was ethnically cleansed of 8,000 souls. That was the year when 169 citizens were slaughtered by a domestic terrorist in Oklahoma City. That was the year when twenty-two people were killed at Beit Lid, Israel, in the first Palestinian suicide bombing.

Malevolent forces also gathered over Cascade City that year, and its magnificent isolation and serene preoccupation could not protect it.

Max (Mountain) Montane turned his vintage, 1975 metallic blue Cadillac into a rest stop overlooking Cascade City. Stumpy Henderson, spat a chewed cigar butt out the window, lit a new corona, and estimated the potential profit of the view below. The two con men were making a hasty, desperate, skin-of-your-teeth escape from Venice California's famed Muscle Beach.

"Now ain't that a pretty sight. That town's ripe for the pickin'. Just like Old Shifty told us. That man knows how to pick a mark." Stumpy spewed billows of black smoke into the undefiled air.

"Looks perfect. This time it'll be the perfect con, in the perfect place. I've worked it five different ways, in five different towns, in five different states. The kinks are out now. And no body'll be able to track us to this hick town. Who'd ever find it?"

Max's ferret eyes took account of the economic assets he saw before him as he mentally licked his chops. He restarted the Cadillac's engine, began his descent and swooped down upon the town; a raptor pursuing his prey. Within the next six months Max and Stumpy insinuated themselves into Cascade City's lives and secret desires. Its hidden weaknesses and unadmitted passions became inflamed and seduced by the hyperbole of the hype.

Max and Stumpy converted an empty warehouse into a makeshift gym. From there the two sociopaths promoted the "Cascade City Development and Expansion Project." The town loved the idea of being part of the fitness craze dominating the country and readily bought into Max's plans. Their town would become the Northwest resort and fitness capitol. The spa's proposed name perfectly fit their fantasies, "Club Mod," trendy and a little exclusive. Stumpy pointed out to every senior citizen that their insurance companies would gladly pay the hefty membership fees. Everyone could see that it was a Win! Win!

The walls of the gym were covered with physical fitness degrees and certifications, the meticulous artwork of Stumpy, master forger. But his masterpieces were the purchased and stolen trophies that he had re-inscribed with fictitious dates and championship titles. Life-sized, enhanced photos of a young "Mountain Montane's" physique lined the entrance, while autographed pictures of movie-star body builders, Arnold Schwarzenegger and Lou Firrigno dazzled the county. From a distance the superimposed imaging was almost flawless. Gaining the confidence of a mark required credibility, authenticity, and expertise. And the town was beginning to feel very confident. They signed check after check to "get the ball rolling."

One freezing morning that fall, forty Club members were working out on new, unpaid for, weight machines and exercise equipment. Whenever bills could no longer be dodged it was time to build vision, so Max was cantillating his tried and true, "Vision Oratorio."

"Partners, all of this," the vulture spun in midair unfurling his wings, "it's only the beginning." Pitching the spin was Max's favorite part of the con. He always believed every lie he told. "Partners, our beautiful city is an uncut gem, an untapped well, an unmined resource. Together we can cut it. We can sink the well and mine the resource. It's the beginning of our world class resort and spa. I'm talking world class! I've built plenty of 'em. That blue Cadillac of mine? Used to belong to Elvis. That's right! None other. A gift from the King himself, God rest his soul." Max looked up, sighing reverently towards heaven.

"We built a resort together—outside of Memphis. The stories I could tell... The Memphis Mafia and me? Just like that." He demonstrated the sacred fairytale with two crossed fingers held high.

"But the resort we're building... It'll be even bigger, grander. Condos. Restaurants, boutiques. Why, even a casino! You've got Indian Tribes around here--with Tribes, the government will build you a casino! Think of the jobs, the property values. I'm talking big bucks here, colleges for your kids… hospitals… help the less fortunate. Partners, dream it and build it!"

Just as Stumpy prepared to rally the crowd, just as Max readied his rhetoric for an additional investment appeal, their past broke through the door. A man with a small, trembling boy behind him exploded into the gym, firing a mail order, semi-automatic AK 47. Bursts of hot lead fire, cold vengeance, and hatred tore off Max's head and cut Stumpy in two.

"You took everything! Our home, our savings, our future. You killed my wife's will to live. You never stopped… until everything was gone…It ends now! You'll never destroy another family or town."

The horrified boy scrambled behind the leg pump machine as, with an agonizing scream, the man turned the weapon on himself.

The names of the 1995 massacres; Beit Lid, Oklahoma City, Srebrenica and Cascade City have receded into history now, but their effects have remained. Devastation and humiliation were for some, a bitter bequest, forever to be mourned and avenged. But for others, The Phoenix Legacy, the power to rise, hidden in every disaster, was released.

After the massacre of Beit Lid, Israel upgraded her defenses keeping the country safe for the next twenty years. Mothers of Srebrenica, Europe's worst genocide since 1945, taught their children forgiveness and not hatred. Their voices challenge the world today with the cry: "Never again." Oklahoma City rebuilt, redesigned, and reinvented itself after the notorious bombing, becoming a security paragon.

Cascade City built a memorial park on the ruins of the illusionary fitness center that hosts regional soccer tournaments and tourist-filled art fairs. The son of "The Cascade City Killer" grew up in his uncle's home and joined the F.B.I. As the highly decorated head of its Frauds & Con Men department, he vindicated many wrongs. And every fall for twenty years he visited Cascade City with his three sons, graduates of West Point, Julliard and The Chicago Art Institute.

Great Oregon Elk-Hunt

By Joe Schrader

An old jail-house buddy of Three-Fingers, Lars Jorgeson, had left our Land of 1,000 Lakes about four or five years ago. He'd found the overly-strict Fish & Game regulations here too heavily enforced. As well as those statutes applying to petty-theft, assault-and-battery, and child-support. After a second conviction for poaching, Lars pulled up stakes and headed west. Minnesota's loss was Oregon's gain. Or vice-versa.

Neither man was much at written communications... leaving school in the eighth grade hinders a polished academic excellence...but Lars telephoned occasionally, always raving about the good hunting. After continued bragging about the plentiful big-game out West, Lars finally convinced Three-Fingers to join him for elk season. Now Three-Fingers had plenty of experience in the woods, mostly stalking deer, snowshoe-rabbits, and various wild-fowl. Something as big as an elk was completely foreign to the Great Lakes area.

"No need to worry about a license, buddy; these Rangers are real lenient. And I'll provide all we need -- rifle, tent, cooking-gear. Just you bring some good warm huntin' clothes; I'll take care of everything else... you betcha'! And be ready for some huge animals; these critters make them itty-bitty Minnesota deer look like midgets."

It was a long three-day bus ride on the Greyhound, but finally Three-Fingers arrived in Madras for the rendezvous with his buddy Lars. Over a huge meal of biscuits-and-gravy and some flapjacks with pork sausage, the two discussed the "safari".

As promised, Lars had brought along a ton of gear... actually enough for eight men for a two-week trek into the wilderness. His rusted-out Ford pickup groaned under the weight, and let out a belch of blue smoke as they headed towards the Ochoco National Forest. A stop for gas (and three quarts of oil) at Prineville, and thence east towards the spot Lars had scouted out for the best "harvest". They passed large ranches of horse and cattle, rocky buttes, and occasional wetlands. The last few miles seemed to be a huge burden on the dilapidated pickup, but finally the pair arrived at an abandoned spring where they'd pitch camp.

"Three-Fingers, this is primo elk territory. Them buggers come down to this spring for water and to munch the nearby pasture. You can hear them 'bugling' all times of day. We got this whole section to ourselves, so relax and get ready for some great shootin' tomorrow! No other hunters...AND no blasted game-wardens to pester us about licenses or such. Buddy, this is my idea of Heaven! Can you give me a refill on that coffee?"

They'd set up a fairly decent bivouac, and Lars had indeed thought of everything. They had a sizeable tent and comfy sleeping-bags, cooking-gear, and guns for them both. Lars had brought his favorite, a 300 Savage, for himself; a Winchester .30-06 would be for Three-Fingers. The heaping big pot of stew, savored around the campfire, filled their stomachs and they retired to the tent. Next morning would begin "The Big Hunt".

Bright and early...well, if you consider 10 AM as 'early'... the pair emerged to a bright sunny day. Lars stoked the campfire and began preparing coffee and bacon-and-eggs. A nearby trench served as their bathroom and after scratching, honking his nose and farting for a few minutes, Three-Fingers joined him.

They left the kitchen mess for later and plunged off into the surrounding forested hills, clad in their brown camouflage hunting outfits. The terrain was much hillier than Three-Fingers was accustomed to, so he was panting heavily after a half-hour hike. They took a break, shared a cigarette and a swallow of blackberry brandy. Well, maybe two swallows...or three. Having spotted absolutely nothing after a two-hour excursion, they headed back to camp for a cheese-sandwich and a beer... and a much-needed nap.

At 4 PM, Lars suggested that since it would be dark soon, maybe they ought to call it a day and continue their quest tomorrow. They agreed as how a game or two of gin-rummy (with a couple more beers) would be fun. Left-over stew and some venison jerky comprised their dinner, and the pair retired early. Lars snored horribly loud, but Three-Fingers dozed off quickly despite the racket. Neither heard the evening bugling of some nearby elk.

Wednesday was a carbon-copy of Tuesday: heavy breathing, farting, a nip or two at the brandy flask, early lunch....and more gin-rummy. No animals of ANY kind were sighted .The weather was turning colder but both denied that any Oregon weather could match their experiences with Minnesota Januarys.

Thursday morning surprised the two when they awoke at 10 AM to a light dusting of snow around their tent. But this would not daunt our fearless duo; off into the woods they tramped. Lars suggested a change of strategy: splitting up to double their chances of spotting an elk. So off they hiked, one north from camp, one south.

Three-Fingers' route took him away from the heavily-wooded section, down a butte towards a green pastured area. The trees thinned out so visibility was better...and walking was not quite so up-and-down.

But some factors were still a constant in his demeanor: scratching, belching, farting...and very heavy breathing. This, mixed with an occasional sip of peppermint Schnapps. The brandy has mysteriously disappeared sometime yesterday.

Suddenly, he spotted his quarry: not fifty yards away stood the largest critter he had ever seen in all his days as a hunter. A dark brown in color, about five feet high at the shoulder, and sporting the longest rack imaginable! This beast was a perfect target, standing broadside to him, stock still...and seemingly unaware of a man's presence.

"Oh, boy!" thought Three-Fingers. "Here's my chance to show that know-it-all Lars. When I bring this baby back to camp maybe he'll quit his infernal bragging. And no time for 'buck-fever' now; got to stop shaking."

BANG!

Quickly, whooping and hollering for all his might, Three-Fingers approached the dead animal. Yep, a perfect shot, right through the chest. Not a quiver as the blood slowly seeped onto the ground. What a monster beast.

He fired three more shots in the air (their secret signal to announce a 'kill') and waited for Lars to join him for the celebration. Within minutes, his buddy had joined him, huffing and puffing. Now we'll see who is Champion Hunter, the master woodsman, the conqueror of the wilderness!

When Lars came to a halt, his jaw dropped. He gazed at the dead critter and turned to his pal with a dazed look. "You idiot! Do you realize what you done killed?!? This ain't no elk, partner; this ain't even a deer. You done gone and shot a long-horned steer! I know there ain't no long-horns in Minnesota, but hain't you ever seed a John Wayne movie? Din't you never watch "Rawhide"? Goldurn it, now we got us a problem."

Yes, friends -- our lads did have a problem indeed. Those three gunshots that Three-Fingers fired? Well, they not only summoned Lars, but also a U.S. government Forest Ranger. He'd heard the international distress-signal of three shots and came to assist. Both the men relinquished their rifles and followed the Ranger to his waiting truck. Proper legal procedures were to follow, over at the courthouse in Bend. One bright note: it was only the first conviction for poaching for Three-Fingers and Lars... at least in Oregon.

Their court-appointed attorney argued that they'd not shot an out-of-season animal, therefore no poaching was committed. The judge denied the motion. But in one aspect, the men were fortunate: no jail time...IF they complied with the terms of their probation. Yep, community-service for our fearless woodsmen --- with a mandatory course in hunter-safety (and wildlife identification as well).

The Day I Met the James Gang

"By Dr. C. C. Mason
As told to the Huntington Herald-Dispatch"

I particularly remember the year—1875—because it happened just before the private telephone line of Francis Hersey was installed so he could communicate between his office at the Chesapeake & Ohio depot and the home where he boarded. Now that was in 1876, so you see why it is easy to remember, being the first telephone so installed.

But that's not the story I want to tell you.

The story I want to tell you is about the day my brother-in-law Ed Howard and I met the James gang. We not only met them, we stood up to them.

Here's how it happened.

I had just gone down the street for my mid-day meal, leaving Ed to mind Murphy's drugstore which we owned together. Now you have to remember that in those days a drugstore was more than a pharmacy. It was more of a general store, actually. We sold everything from kitchen towels to liniment to baby diapers. I was the actual druggist; trained and certified in the Medical Register of the United States. Ed was the manager.

We also sold whisky, but you had to have a prescription for that. No prescription, no whisky. That's the way it was in Huntington, West Virginia. And that's an important part of this story.

As I said, I was out having my meal when the James gang rode into town on horseback, right up to the front of our store on Guyan Street.

Now this next part is told by Ed.

He says two of the men alighted, strode boldly into the store and asked for the druggist. That would have been me. Those James boys wanted a pint of whiskey. Ed had to tell them I was out—that must have taken a bit of nerve—and those two turned away, disappointed Ed could tell you!

Just about that moment, I returned and heard that they wanted whisky. I asked for their prescription, which they related to me they did not have. You remember I said this was an important part.

I declined to sell them the whisky. Stood right up to them I did.

Ed was by my side and he thought it might be a good idea to sell them something—after all a customer is a customer—so he asked would they like some cigars. They allowed as how they wouldn't mind a few cigars, so Ed sold them five Black Diamonds at ten cents each.

The James boys nodded, turned and rejoined their companions waiting outside, restless astride their dusty horses. Then they all galloped away—to rob the Bank of Huntington!

By Susan Springer Munger

chanticleer point

By Mary Jane Nordgren

angry pines
evergreens spurred
to shrieking fury
by cock rooster winds
charging the cliffs
of columbia gorge
in bright february sky
peregrine staggers
across invisible currents
veering south
from intended east
too buffeted and chilled
to fight this day
chanticleer's
clear screech of
dominance

Disaster in the North Sea

By Mitch Metcalf

The wind howled and filled the air with salt spray which joined the cold rain and splattered hard on anything it could find to hit, making a sharp sound like a bug colliding with the windshield of a car. The Arctic wind was fierce and bitter cold and tested all things that fought to resist, making sure that anything not securely tied down would instantly learn to fly.

It was late March and the short days of winter were behind, but still when the sun went down the day gave way to the long black nights like a lid clamping down on a cold iron pot. This was the middle of the North Sea, one of the most ferocious bodies of water on the planet. Today the swells were moderate, only thirty-five feet or so. A month ago they'd been hitting ninety feet. Regardless of size, the swells came hard and fast. This was dangerous water to be in.

Torg Gundersen was fit, tall, fair-skinned, blue-eyed, a classic Norwegian. Blond hair peeked out around his colorful knit cap. He had been working here for months, doing eight day shifts, twelve hours a day, along with 200 other men, to build an oil rig in the North Sea. The Edda C was a permanent oil rig that rose up from the ocean floor, 300 feet below the surface, to well over 100 feet above the water. The rig was coming along nicely, but still lacked living quarters and a kitchen, so every evening, the crew would leave the rig by walking across a gangplank, put into place by a crane, and over to the Alexander Kjelland, a floating hotel, anchored next to the Edda. The men knew not to wear loose fitting clothing. This wind could fill it like a sail and launch a man over the railing.

Once in the water, you had about four minutes before the cold would render your arms and legs useless and you'd sink out of sight into the steely grey.

The Alexander Kjelland was originally a floating oil rig, designed to do drilling work in shallow coastal areas, but had been pressed into service to become a floating hotel, a 'flotel', for the men. It was a pentagon shaped, five-legged platform whose first deck level stood ninety feet above the water. Each leg had a massive pontoon under it that could be made more or less buoyant by adding water, and an 18 ton anchor holding each in its place.

The crew quarters were basically steel shipping containers that had been converted to living quarters and stacked on top of each other, four men to a room, six rooms to a container, four containers to a stack, and enough stacks to house 240. Doors, hallways and stairs were added to connect everything and, presto, you had a hotel. The original structures of the rig contained the dining area, kitchen and multipurpose rooms, used for meetings and movies.

Torg, having just finished dinner, was joining his friends Collin Buchanon and Lars Andersen, who were also welders, in the movie room. The men had become good friends here, but lived far apart when they went home. Collin was from Norwich, England, Lars from Stavanger, Norway and Torg from Kristiansand, Norway. The crews were brought together from many different places and most commuted to the western coastal city of Stavanger, Norway by commercial air-craft. Once there, they would make their way to the Heliport in Tananger and take a three-hour helicopter trip out to the rigs. About 50 rigs had been built since oil had been discovered in the North Sea twenty years earlier. Torg walked into the spacious movie room and searched the rows of stacking chairs for his friends.

The movie room, with its eight-foot ceiling, measured about twenty by forty feet. The metal walls were not the greatest for acoustics; those unlucky to sit far left or right had a terrible view of the screen and could barely hear the movie. Luckily, he had his friends holding a seat for him near the center of the room.

As he approached, Collin motioned him over to the seat between him and American Jim Stevens, the maintenance supervisor. Jim, a bearded, stickily-built man who had worked all over the world, told many stories that the Norwegians enjoyed.

The movie was about to begin when everyone abruptly sat upright and listened. A loud sound...a kind of crack... and now the room was trembling. Suddenly the floor began tilting left; the chairs began sliding, tangling men, chairs and equipment. The projector crashed down. Within moments, the floor tilted to 30 degrees and as men and chairs were heaped against the wall amid loud thumps and chaotic crashing sounds.

The men knew something disastrous had happened, but had no way of knowing that one of the legs of the platform had broken completely off, and that the shuddering they felt was the eighteen-ton anchor on the opposite leg dragging across the bottom of the ocean floor until it finally caught, stopping the rig from flipping over.

Torg slammed open a locker containing lifejackets and hurriedly put one on. He then fought his way outside, ducking and squinting as the cold wind and spray blasted his skin. He could see that most of the men were making their way up to the highest point of the rig, to his right. To his left, he could see the dark water of the North Sea was much too close.

Stepping out through the door, Torg lost his grip and footing at the same time and slid. He'd barely registered the shocking cold as he was pulled under the water when a swell swung a large metal container around on top of him. The container pinned him, but did not crush him. Torg strained against the weight but could not budge it. The surface was a mere arm's length away, but he knew he was never going to reach it.

"This is it," he thought. "I'm not going to be able to take another breath. I'm about to die."

Another swell lifted the container off of him and he scrambled up and filled his lungs with air. Torg managed to grab a railing to pull himself up and out of the water. On the sloping deck, Torg could see many men fighting the wind to make their way to the highest point.

The American Jim Stevens, reacting quickly, had made his way to the nearest lifeboat. He helped two dozen other men get onboard and then pulled the launch lever. Once free of the dock clamps, the boat swung out hard at an angle, causing the cable to jam the winch. Unable to go up or down, the boat swung in the wind, fifty feet above the water.

Jim and Torg, who was nearing the high point of the floundering flotel, heard the anchor cable snap. With a sharp crack, the cable released the pent up energy of hundreds of thousands of pounds of pressure and whipped back, slicing through a dozen men in its path. Lars Andersen was in this group and died instantly.

With no anchor holding it, the flotel completed its flip and all aboard were now in the water and being sucked down by the submerging rig.

Torg was tumbled into the frigid water. The lower he was pushed, the darker it got. Again he was sure his time was up.

With his air nearly depleted, he suddenly realized he could see light above him. The life vest was bringing him up to the surface! He kicked with all his might, praying he would get there before he passed out. He wasn't sure he was going to make it.

Jim and the others who had been dangling above the water in the lifeboat now found themselves pulled below the surface by the unreleased cable. As the flotel sank, their lifeboat was hauled down with it. They were now completely under water and upside down.

The sturdy craft had been designed to survive oil field disasters. It could be buttoned-up tight enough to go through burning oil fires and had an interior air tank that could keep the inside air pressure higher than the outside air pressure so no smoke would get into the cabin. It was designed to right itself if rough seas flipped it. These features kept the craft from filling with water and also righted the boat, which let it break free of the cable that had been dragging it down.

At the surface, Jim Stevens opened the sliding window cover to look outside, scanning the water for men. When Torg rose, coughing and sputtering, he was no more than five feet from the boat. The two men locked eyes. With the window fully open, it was wide enough for two men to lean out and grab Torg. They pulled him and another nineteen men out of the water that night.

The date was March 27, 1980. Of the 212 men on the Alexander Kjelland, 123 perished. This was the worst maritime disaster in Norwegian waters since WWII.

SEEDS OF...

SECTION II – RELATING

Listening to Beethoven's Sixth

by Fred Melden

The deaf man composes
and the lame make their way
through life; and hard hats stack
skyscraper floors for the many
doings they do not understand.
And hordes of pedestrian minds
open their hearts
so clichés will not be homeless.

Some woman
with a hollow body
transformed the dusky paper marks
to my tremolo morning. And would she
have drawn the bow with the flow
of the brook except for the man
who loved the grain of tangible things?
I'm sure he has heard her too –
and perhaps the Jack who trekked
from the other side of the tracks
to drop the tree in the forest. But even if deaf
when he swung that inkless axe
there still would have been these sounds.
We orbit around each other and must not cease
the universe has no center.

Gray on Gray

By Roger G. Ritchey

She gradually ... became form
Allowed by a thin wind
Piercing yellow eyes fixed on two objects
First, her primary prey,
Then me
The dense fog was blanketing
Water dripping like rain
The slight breeze was blowing
From me to her
So ... she had known
Of my presence
But her hunger
And demanding pups
Pushed relentlessly
For food
I retreated
To hopefully allow
Her seizure of the rodent
Then came
The long, graceful pounce

The audible snap
A muted tiny shrill
And violent shake
To snap
The gopher's neck
Another glance at me

And perhaps
A look of triumph,
Purely primordial
She turned to me
Once more
Then
Was again
Wrapped in fog
Gray on gray
We became friends
In a remote way
Through her morning ritual
That included a pass
Through apple trees and meadow

Then the neighbor
Playing the Big White Hunter
A single shot
Destroyed the den

Succulent

By Hannah Thuku Kolehmainen

My thoughts of you are redolent
Of a battered desert succulent.
On your spiny, scarred exterior

Lovers, long broken up, etched their undying love.
What did that have to do with you?

How faithfully you stay in place
When burning heat seeks to displace
Eliminate you, leave no trace

To tell you that your faith's misplaced.
When doubts assail you, foes abound
You hunker down and stand your ground
Your unseen wells of sustenance
Cause you to smile and even dance.

You are worn yet beautiful,

Dry yet refreshing

Spent yet nourishing.

Succulent in every way.

Shotzy

By B. R. Walker

Earl looked even smaller than he was, standing handcuffed between his lawyer and the police officer as the judge pronounced his verdict. He was remanded to the custody of a home for the mentally ill in the city thirty miles away, one especially for senior citizens. My heart went out to him. It's true that he'd evidenced outrageous behavior toward other residents of the assisted living facility where he'd been for over two years, including a violent outburst against a woman in a wheelchair. That got him arrested and landed him in court, but I was heartsick that the even greater restrictions of his now court-ordered next home were necessary.

I'd been his money manager for about those same two years. He'd never expressed any out-of-the-way behavior toward me, but I was well aware of some legitimate complaints against him and wondered if even greater confinement would only make him more volatile—except for one thing—Shotzy.

Earl had had his little black and white mutt since it was a pup. They adored each other. I was sure Earl would be worse, and that they'd both suffer deeply if parted. I said a small prayer, and it was answered. Earl would be in a ten-bed ward and could take only such personal items as would fit into one narrow locker—and Shotzy. In a surprise blessing the manager of the mental health facility had visited Earl, met Shotzy and said okay to his bringing the dog along. It seems she too owned a dog very much like him.

The hearing ended. I moved to the front of the courtroom. The Social Services Rep told Earl she'd move his clothes. The police officer stood ready to escort him away. "And Shotzy?" he mumbled. "What about my Shotzy?" The social worker waved her hand and turned to leave. "Oh, I don't know anything about that," she said, and was gone. Earl's face fell.

"I'll bring Shotzy, Earl," I said. "Don't worry."

The policeman whisked him away.

Back at the assisted living facility, I inquired about Shotzy. Nobody knew where he was, but, since Earl's arrest, Shotzy was given the run of the two-story, hundred-apartment building. He could be anywhere! The pet of no one was the pet of everyone, taking handouts from anyone and of anything offered. Just as I voiced my dismay, the fluff of a mutt bounced around a corner and waggled up to me. I was no stranger to him and easily picked him up, said good-byes and headed for my car. As I put him in the passenger seat beside me his mood noticeably changed. To my knowledge, he'd rarely, if ever, been in a car, and his apprehension was apparent. I pulled out, continually reassuring him this thirty mile trip was going to be okay in the end, but he remained concerned. So six miles down the road I pulled into a drive-in and ordered us each a hamburger. His plain, mine with the works. After blowing on it to cool it down, I set the meat on the seat, and he eagerly went to work. That helped. He sat quietly at attention for the rest of the trip, watching carefully every turn.

We hit big city traffic. It took concentration and a couple wrong tries before I found the address. Amidst a maze of narrow streets, the old three-story Victorian house stood on a corner in a rather dismal neighborhood of like-minded ladies who'd seen better days. They towered shoulder to shoulder with lots of steps elevating their lace-collared facades, reminding me of very long-nosed, superior beings. The effect was softened by lots of big trees ruffling the sidewalks and effectively hiding house numbers. I had to park a block away.

Shotzy bounced up and down on the seat as I tried to fasten his leash. "Okay, okay, fella, end of the line, simmer down."

As I opened the door, he leapt out and at a dead run headed across the street and down the block towards the right house, pulling me after him at uncustomary speed!

"Whoa! Hey, guy, wait up!"

He made a beeline for the long flight of steps and dragged me up to the front door.

"What the heck, you've been here before!" I caught my breath and rang the bell. We were greeted by a nurse who inquired for I.D. Shotzy straining on his leash to get into the place made digging for my driver's license an acrobatic endeavor. Finally the nurse cleared us and we were admitted.

As I stepped over the sill, Shotzy tore away from me and skittered down the long hall, tripping over himself, the leash, and a couple attendants before leaping, waggling and whimpering with joy, into Earl's arms. The man burst into tears. I could have cried, too. I left them to their hugging and licking and followed the manager to her office.

Shotzy would sleep under Earl's hospital bed. A blanket and food dishes were ready for him there. Yes, she truly understood how much it meant for Earl to have Shotzy with him. Because of his age and health, the prognosis for Earl ever being released were very dim. He'd never had any children and either outlived or alienated any friends or family.

At least none were known. But Shotzy would jump in his lap with his tail wagging, and Earl's black moods softened as he hugged his little dog. I had to inquire: had Earl or Shotzy ever been here before? No, the manager said, and she'd been there many years. I shook my head in wonderment. I had no doubt somehow Shotzy knew Earl was here.

A couple years later I heard that Earl had died. My first thought was, "What about Shotzy?" I was told that they kept him. The understanding manager took care of his needs. He became the mascot for the whole place, and I'm sure that wagging mop of a dog brought to many other troubled minds something of just what unconditional love is all about.

There is a bumper sticker that always reminds me of these two. It says, "Lord, help me be the person my dog thinks I am."

I don't know how Shotzy knew which house Earl was in, but he did.

I don't know why that small dog cared so much for that angry, troubled man, but he did.

Maybe, just maybe, under all the anger and turmoil Shotzy saw who Earl really was, or who he could be and somehow touched that.

Or maybe, just maybe, that little dog know all there was to know about Earl and loved him anyway.

Or maybe Shotzy only saw the part of Earl that loved him in return, and that was enough. I don't know.

I do know there is a love that transcends all time and space, all anger and even evil, to wrap each of us in its arms and hold us close every now and then. We need to remember that and try to return it as much as we are able, even when the source is just a little mutt of a dog. And when we do, it comes back to us in even greater measure, no matter what has gone on before. I know this because, in spite of a mind which often disappeared into unknown depths unacceptable to the rest of us, Earl still loved that little dog and Shotzy loved the man in return. And I know it because even while Earl was miles and miles away in the midst of a big city teeming with thousands and thousands of people, and even if he couldn't get to him on his own, Shotzy knew exactly where Earl was. That kind of love will always know where you are.

El Pollo Loco

By Rebecca Robinson

Once a caged chicken barely able to move
she'd been set free to sow her wild grits
pluck whoever she wanted
wild and free-range old biddy

Being single felt more like a fox in the hen house
She wanted more than to cock-a-doodle do
She brooded and she slept
some nights she even wept
Dense, dusty road full of ruts and rocks
In the scattered fodder she discovered a scruffy rooster

Who shared his chicken feed with her
combed her ruffled feathers smooth
gave her long, luxurious dust baths
lulled her to sleep in the comfort of her chicken coop
made her feel like a chick again

Brought new meaning to a good ol' chicken scratch
listening intently to all her clucking
enjoying her crazy, full-throttled laughter
with no embarrassment
no threats to wring her neck
bestowing her with hugs and pecks

Feels like the Cock of the Walk
when he struts with her 'til the crack of dawn
where she finds nothing stuck in her craw
loving his faded wattles and his fine white down
Sunny warm and hushed secure on a wing and a prairie

Am I Akin to Earth?

By Barbara Schultz

I am the dark soil.
I am the sprouting seed.
I am the cold and the ice.
I am the snow falling gently.
I am the wind whipping branches.
I am the tiny green frog living under the leaf,
    unseen.
I am the slug, the worm, the beetle.
What am I not?
I become one with, I savor and delight,
Know myself larger, smaller,
A tiny particle
    In this great
        World, this universe.
            I merge and lose myself.

Chipmunks Make the Best Friends

By G. A. Meyerink

The park bench was deserted when Alicia sat down. She wanted someplace quiet to eat her lunch and reflect on the news she had received that morning. The tall pines sheltered the bench from the summer sun, whose warmth released the tangy fragrance of the trees. Alicia took a deep refreshing breath, then a bite of her sandwich.

As the crumbs from her meal fell into her lap, she casually brushed them off onto the needle-strewn grounds. She was focusing on her thoughts, so she didn't notice the small scurrying animals for several minutes. In fact, she didn't notice them at all until a deep male voice said, "Your busy little guests are looking for more handouts."

Startled, Alicia looked up into clear twinkling blue eyes set in a strong, handsome face. "Hello, may I join you? I have something these chipmunks would enjoy, too."

Alicia nodded her assent. She could hardly tell him to go away – it was a public bench. She turned her attention to the begging animals and tossed them the last crust of her meal. The stranger was silent for a few minutes, casually tossing nuts to the now ecstatic rodents.

"Chipmunks always remind me of summers at the old family cabin," the man said. "We fed them every day and gave them names."

Alicia did not respond. She was not sure she wanted to be drawn into conversation with this man.

"They are very accepting of humans, as long as we don't threaten them," he said. "They must think you are pretty safe."

Alicia looked over at the man again. He seemed "safe", too, and she suddenly needed to talk.

"I don't feel safe," she said. "I feel pretty much beaten up, figuratively," she added. Then she spilled all she had been thinking about since she had heard the news that morning.

The man listened quietly. Alicia felt better just getting her thoughts out in the open They did not seem as dismal in the sunlight. She found it easy to tell him about Lucas, about how long she had wanted to date him, and how excited she had been when he first called her.

"It took a few months, but by now I thought we were a couple. I was sure he felt the same way. He acted as if we were meant to be together." Alicia sniffled and started to wipe her nose on her lunch bag.

The man handed her a tissue.

"And then, and then…, and THEN," Alicia sobbed, "I just heard he's getting MARRIED on Saturday!"

Alicia's outburst had scattered the chipmunks into bushes and under leaves. The kindly gentleman at her side handed her another tissue and tossed a few peanuts at the frightened animals to appease them.

"Humph, sounds like a real cad to me."

"You're right. He is a cad. That's such a good word for him," Alicia almost smiled in relief. "He's a cad," she reemphasized to herself. "He's a cad!" she repeated more strongly. "HE'S A CAD AND I AM BETTER OFF WITHOUT HIM!"

Alicia turned to her companion and smiled. "Thanks. That felt good. I'm Alicia, by the way." She offered her hand.

"My name is Ralph," he said, graciously accepting her hand and returning her smile. His shock of snow white hair fell across his forehead and the creases around his friendly eyes tightened as he smiled back at her. His hand was dotted with age spots and his fingers were knobby.

"My sister once met a cad like that," Ralph mused. "Father was about to take the shotgun after him but Mother persuaded him not to. Good thing – my sister married a much better man a few months later. They were married for 45 happy, pleasant years," Ralph added softly.

Alicia gazed thoughtfully at her new friend. She wanted to stay on the bench and visit with him longer. His face promised a treasure source of wisdom and experience which she felt she desperately needed.

As if he understood her unasked question, Ralph said, "I come here every day to feed the chipmunks. They are about the only friends I have left now."

"Oh!" Alicia exclaimed. "You have me! I mean, if you don't mind. I'd love to feed the chipmunks with you."

"That would be nice," Ralph said. "Is this a good time for you?"

"This time …oh! Time!" Alicia looked at her watch and hurriedly gathered her belongings. "I have to get back to work! Yes, this time tomorrow." She rushed off, turning at the corner to wave at the old man on the bench.

Alicia and Ralph met often for lunch and to feed the chipmunks. They even gave some of them names that suited their busy personalities. 'Pouchy' would sit on his haunches and beg for more food, even with his cheek pouches stuffed full. 'Noisy' chattered constantly, 'Stripe' had an extra wide stripe along his back and 'Lucas' brazenly stole food from the others. "He's a cad," Alicia explained when she named him.

The summer and fall passed quickly. Ralph listened patiently to Alicia's recitals of humorous events at work and her descriptions of her current dates. He told her about dating when he was young and his adventures driving around the country before super highways and ubiquitous gas stations. The chipmunks grew fatter.

On a chilly Monday noon Alicia sat shivering on the bench. Most of the chipmunks were gone. She decided they would have to meet indoors next time, and she tried to think where a good place would be. Ralph was late. That was unusual. Most days he was waiting for her to arrive.

Soon a neatly dressed woman sat on the bench. She looked just a bit older than Alicia and something around her eyes suggested great sorrow. Alicia wanted to tell her to leave, the spot was reserved, but she hesitated. This woman needed a friend, and Ralph would be a good friend for her, too.

The woman turned to Alicia and in a gentle voice said, "My name is Catherine. Are you Alicia?"

Startled, Alicia could only nod.

"Ralph said I would find you here. He was my grandfather."

Alicia heard the "was" and could only stare at the woman.

"Grandfather Ralph passed away last night. He wanted me to tell you. He said you were the best friend he had, and he did not want you to be lonely." Catherine pulled a small brown bag from her tote. "I brought my lunch. I hope we can be friends, too."

Pouchy scurried out from under some dry leaves and sat expectantly in front of Alicia. It looked as if he, too, was waiting for her answer.

"Sure," said Alicia. "I'd like that."

Thoughts

By William L. Stafford

Got up today dressed and went to my home office.
Reached up to the shelf above my computer to retrieve the
pitcher of thoughts I keep there.
I grab a cup and carefully pour it nearly full of thoughts, being
careful not spill any; if they happen to soak the blotter
it could be world-changing without my knowledge.
I ponder how to proceed. 10 seconds in the microwave to give
a warm fuzziness to what is to come. A minute or more in the
microwave would cause a too-steamy outcome probably.
In the fridge? Oh, no, not into cold ruminations today.
Maybe add something from the cupboard. I stand to retrieve
one of the bottles from my dictionary and pick 15. Just a
half teaspoon of words starting with the letter "O". I add
it and give it a quick stir. I lift the cup to my nose and sniff,
to see if there has been any aroma added with the "O" words.
Oleander attacks my senses and a brilliant picture enters my
head of the garden party in Pakistan where I attended
the installation of an ambassador at the embassy there.
Time for a small taste. I sip carefully, do not need an overdose.
Occasional oblong octagonal objects occur often on Orion
orbits. What, where the heck did that come from?
I might need to rethink how to proceed. Another small sip.
Over objection of official officers observe obtuse onslaught.
Octopus opts out of Olympics.

I can see this is not going to work out. I grab a baggie and pour the rest of the thought from the pitcher into it. Sealing it tight, I label it and store it among the other random thought days that I seem to collect on a regular basis. Tomorrow is another day. I definitely will not use the Orange cup again. The cup probably caused the thing to go off the rails. It is possible I should refrain from stirring.

Hitchhikers?

By Joan (Michalke) Ritchey

I walked out of the Hillsboro Eye Clinic more despondent than ever. My macular degeneration was progressing. In fact, my right eye was very near unseeing, not to mention that I now had the beginnings of cataracts. 'But,' exclaimed the ophthalmologist, 'with your glasses, you have 20/20 vision in your left eye, so you can still drive.'

'Wow! I wonder if he really knows what I am NOT seeing.' The thought ran through my mind as I made my way to my car.

I spotted my old Nash Rambler. You couldn't miss it for its garish pink hood and matching sides with white rooftop—my main reason for keeping it because today's automobile styles and colors are so boringly similar.

I approached hesitantly. I thought I had locked the doors—was sure I had! But two silhouetted figures appeared to be seated in the back seat. Just seeing things, I mused. The eye drops administered to dilate my pupils probably haven't worn off.

As I neared my auto, movement in the rear seat confirmed my fears—two figures were sitting there.

I opened my driver's door and was immediately assaulted by a pungent odor. The stale smell, like old clothes worn way too many days in a row, permeated my nostrils.

I looked around for help—none! In a loud voice—just in case someone was within ear shot—I demanded, "What are you doing in my car? Get out!" I shouted.

"Oh please! We were hoping to take a ride. It's such a nice day," said the raspy voice of an old fellow wearing a gray brimmed, crumpled hat. "My name is Ben and this is my friend, Charlie. We mean you no harm and hope you are 'going our way.' We haven't been for a ride in a long time. We travel mainly on foot these days. We figured the car—old as it is—would belong to perhaps a senior citizen."

"Do you live here in Hillsboro?" I asked, still standing outside the vehicle.

"No. We live out of town a ways."

"Well," I said as I took my seat behind the wheel. "I'm on my way home to Forest Grove. I guess I can give you a lift. However, I need to warn you that my eyesight is not very good these days. I have macular degeneration and perhaps my ten-minute wait for the eye drops to wear off was not quite long enough, because the sunlight is very bright. Furthermore, I'm not in the habit of giving hitchhikers a ride."

"Thanks," said Charlie as he raised his hand and doffed the bill of his black and orange baseball cap in my direction, while flashing a broad smile.

Hmm! He can't be too bad. By the insignia on the cap he's sporting—it looks like he's a fan of the OSU Beavers.

"My team, too!" I smiled, peering at him in the rearview mirror. "You guys let me know where you want out, okay?" I asked as I began making my way out of the clinic parking lot.

As I drove through town along SW Baseline, the two old gents jabbered continually, pointing out different buildings and sights, and reminiscing about 'how things used to look.' I approached TV Highway without incident, until…

"Whoa, little lady," shouted Charlie. "That's a red light up there."

I knew the stoplight was there by the cemetery on my right, but I had a hard time focusing with my limited field of vision and glaring sunlight. My tires screeched to a halt.

"Thanks." I muttered.

We made it to the outskirts of Cornelius with only a few honking horns, which seemed to be happening much more frequently of late from drivers who, I figured, had grown impatient traveling so slow behind 'this old lady.'

About halfway through Cornelius…

"Watch Out!" Ben screamed. "There's a car over here. You'd better wait until it passes before you try to switch lanes."

Whew! That was a near miss. "Thanks, Ben."

Then!

"There's a pedestrian up ahead—a young lady pushing a stroller. Better stop until she's out of the crosswalk!" Ben continued.

I watched as she crossed hesitantly in front of me and then I proceeded on my way once she had made it safely to the sidewalk.

On the outskirts of Cornelius—near the new Wal-Mart shopping mall—a young boy on a bicycle sprang into sight and I was reproached again to "be careful."

I moved back into the left lane successfully and drove through the green light at Mountain View Lane. Then I cautiously veered into the left turn lane and proudly waited for the left turn arrow before making my entrance onto Highway #47.

My two hitchhikers still had not said anything about where they wanted to be dropped off, or just where they were going.

Well, they seem to be enjoying their ride! I smiled.

"I'm not going as far as Gaston." I said as I glanced at them in the rearview mirror. I live in Dilley and we only have a couple more miles to go before I reach home," I stated, hoping for a reply, but there was none from either of them.

Driving along Highway #47, near Maple Street, Charlie warned. "You're too close to the center line, Joan. Be careful of the oncoming cars."

I shrugged my shoulders at my two "back seat" drivers as I jerked back into my own lane of traffic. I ignored the motorist as he laid on his horn much too long after he had passed.

Hmm, hadn't I introduced myself as Mrs. Ritchey?

Almost home now, I continued through the flashing yellow light at String-town Road, and then turned right onto my Hiatt Road exit.

I parked in our driveway. Turning, I asked—"Well, fellows, wha…"

The back seat was empty!

They were gone!

The interior musty odor cleared from my nostrils as I exited my car.

Looking skyward… I paused and gave an upward nod and grin before making my way up the front steps to the porch—Home safe!

The Rainbow Curse

By Matthew Hampton

Colors fill the world
with vibrant reds, quiet blues, bright yellows.
Most persons can see colors and rainbows, but not everyone.
Nobody knows how the rainbow curse
chooses someone to leave
with the colorful world faded into dull grays.
Without the colors in the world,
a cursed person can feel like less of a person. Without colors,
cursed persons lose hope easily—even blame themselves
for being cursed.
From their gray world, they can only struggle
to find a rainbow powerful enough
to give them back their colors.
Everyone has a different rainbow, and each hides in dark,
        unexplored places.
It takes time, endurance
but if cursed persons finds their rainbow,
the gray will peel off the world's surface
and colors will shine in their eyes again.
It can be hard. Many give up
before they get to their rainbow.
You may have heard of them.
You might be one of them.
The Rainbow Curse can get anyone.

The Sound of Her Sweet Snore

By Ross M. Hall

There is a soft sound.
You set a piece of pine or fir
Marked for a cut, upon saw horses,
Place the handsaw on the mark,
Drawing the saw back a few inches,
On the place to cut.

This is the sound of her sweet snore.
The harsh sound of the power stroke of the saw
Never comes.
Instead a tender, almost silent exhale,
Then she marks the next cut and repeats,
Reminding me it is time that I also sleep.

I Shot an Arrow...

By Joe Schrader

"I shot an arrow into the air,
It fell to earth I know not where."
— Henry Wadsworth Longfellow

I sent forth this barbed attack, a stout shaft of bitterness
With a piercing point dipped in venom and rancor
Take that!
The returning volley consisted of powder-puff missiles,
Colored with compassion and civility.
Not what I expected; a gentle riposte, not a bombardment.
Screaming a hateful battle-cry, I let loose a potent
          counter-attack:
Plague and disease, reinforced with angry pain.
Once more, my assault was repulsed by an uncharacteristic
Rebuttal: soothing, healthful medicine; an antidote
Tempered with calm.
My third attempt must surely conquer any opposition.
I let loose with poverty and desolation, all the
Negativity my Forces could muster.
This time, as before, those arrows failed to achieve victory.
A bright cornucopia, overflowing with wealth and charity,
Was granted in retaliation.
My martial bugle-call was echoed by a heavenly chorus.
My arsenal was depleted, my armory emptied of all
The Devil's weapons.
Angels never wage war like I do —
But somehow the victory is always theirs.

We Talked of War

by Paula Sheller Adams

In the kitchen by the washer we talked
of war and what gets killed in killing
and what makes enemies.

A bad time to ask such things –
you, on your first leave, home to see your girl.
Due back at base on Monday.
You say it started there beside the washer:
the talk you later had with your commander,
the careful explanation—
You would accept the danger, not the killing,
a medic, yes, but not to carry weapons.
Then came the disbelief, the threats,
the disciplines, the brig and then a trial.
Eventual discharge
stamped dishonorable.

It gives one pause to think what words can do
or have a part in doing –
words said in some crumb of time,
words long ago forgotten.
Then suddenly we come upon them,
rooted and blooming
with all the colors of another soul upon them

and in them see some transformed
fragment of ourselves, emigrated to
more receptive earth.

I have no memory of that time
there in the kitchen by the washer.

Untitled

by Joan Graves

You bring out the gymnast in me
You bring out the Oxsana Baiul
The petite fairy
The tiny dancer

You bring out the athlete
toned and disciplined
with amazing endurance
The Olga Korbut
The Nadia Comaneci
Girls lying about their ages
to compete in contests
to glorify a repressive government

You bring out the doll in me
The Anna Pavlova
Light as a feather
The pert cute child
The jewelry box dancer
The miniature adult

If This was a Movie

By Everett E. Goodwin

If this was a movie
people would have their fingers
in a bag of popcorn

If this was a movie suspense would be mounting.
If this was a movie, the chase scene would be brief.
At first, I'd be chasing you, then you'd be chasing me
Then it would get all mixed up, so that it would be hard to tell

If this was a movie, we would have crossed paths
on the Orient Express, or some exotic bar.
Any sensible producer would have flatly rejected a health
club.
I would have said "How long have you been traveling?"
Instead of "How long have you been a member?"

Come to think of it a lot of our getting together
was just like a movie. Does that mean we have to
wait 'til the last reel to walk into the sunset

swearing eternal devotion.

Seeds of... Music

By Charles E. Pritchard, D.O.

Dat-Dat-Dat-Dah—a simple little letter in Morse Code, from which Beethoven took and wrote a famous symphony. Dat-Dat-Dat Dah. He took the letter V and used it, experienced it, and expanded it to demonstrate the feeling of pride and exhortation of people upon finding out the result of a great battle. Dat-Dat Dat Dah. It stirs the heart of people both then and now with its simple but profound movement. Is this a seed of music? Yes, but is this the only kind?

I know a lovely young lady who has taken music and performed it, written it, and taught it. Is this a seed of music? She has gotten up early, gone to school, and taught many subjects, including music in the forms of band, orchestra, theory and choir, from large groups of 150, to ensembles of four to five and soloists. Some performances were joy to the ears of those fortunate to hear them, while others brought tears to the eyes of the performers' parents, who smiled anyway. She has directed "This Little Light of Mine" with the youngest, to some truly fantastic classical pieces for the adult choir. Has she done this for the money or the applause of an adoring public? No, she has done this to plant the seeds of music in the hearts and souls of those around her. Some seeds fall on barren ground. Some fall on truly rich loam and develop into some magnificent performers. While most fall on soil that is almost OK. And when it grows, it supplies for most and even me the blessings of music, be it song, dance, or instrumental. These, for me, are the true seeds of music.

The Old Mantle Clock

By Joan (Michalke) Ritchey

The fireplace mantle in Grandma's house
Was my earliest memory
Of the old mahogany clock
Whenever I'd visit Grandma
I'd watch her wind it with a key
(I think she waited just for me)

One Spring day the Old Mantle Clock
Came to our homeplace
Through teary eyes I watched my Mom
Set it on our mantle
In its readied space

Tears streaked down Mom's cheeks
As she wound the clock
With Grandma's bright brass key
Mom stood for a long time
Staring at the mantle clock
And only turned around to me
After the clock had chimed
The hour... three
"This clock
Will be yours someday," Mom said
(Grandma's last thoughts were of me)

I never wanted that Old Mantle Clock
I knew the sad news
It would bear THAT day

So, when the cancer
Claimed Mom's life
I stowed the clock away

Time passed and I began
To miss the sound
Of the clock's ticking
And melodic hourly chime
So I retrieved the old clock
Set it on my mantle
Wound it with Grandma's key
And set the time

Now, the only sound
That breaks the silence
In my early hours
Between midnight and dawn
When insomnia
Has robbed me of my sleep
And I find it impossible
To slumber on…
Is the *tick, tick, ticking*

Of the Old Mantle Clock

I ponder about the memories
That old timepiece has recorded
If that face could only speak
Sad times, true…
But happy celebrations, too
When laughter was at its peak.

Birth

By D. K. Lubarsky

Morning air shivers with the smell of birth
Blood, tears, joy, anticipation
My eyes hug the globe of mother and child
I lean closer, to watch the rise and fall of Talia's chest
    … half a hand width in size.

I inhale her exhale, weighing her life force
One day,
      and she has already surpassed her greatest Challenge
She has survived.
Life, love, endless possibilities await
Her little body smells of hope.
Talia's eyes open and the world brightens.

I love you

By D. K. Lubarsky

I love you
    Spoken – face to face
    Whispered – when you sleep
    Dreamed – when I sleep
    Written – on holiday cards, letters, emails
    Heard – across telephone wires
    Penned – in chocolate frosting on birthday cakes
    Celebrated – at marriages, anniversaries and new
    births
    Cried – at death and passings
    Hoped – on long voyages and army deployments
I love you
What does it mean?
    For this second, we are bound together … soul to
    Soul
    A tendril of cosmic energy connects us
I love you
    I see you
    I hear you
    Your imperfections fall like chips of peeling paint,
Revealing the essence of your being.
And I see only the goodness of the universe in your eyes,
Your touch heals and makes me whole
I love you
Miracle of life.

Seeds of...

Section III – Finding Self

Not Yet a Firefly

By Eva Foster

I welcomed the evenings. Peace settled over all things. Confusing events of the day became less important. I liked endings and beginnings; something fresh about both. Evenings were an ending in the hope that maybe tomorrow would be a new beginning.

In Ohio, Midwest summer evenings always held the promise of fireflies. The sun was disappearing and these tiny lightning bugs proved to be a welcome distraction for a ten year old. My sister and I had come to live with Mr. and Mrs. Tarr after grandma died. The Tarr family had known Dad and Mom in their early marriage before Mom had been taken away. All I remember about Mom leaving, were men in white coats and me jumping on her suitcase so I could help get it shut. Dad was a boilermaker and his job meant travel, sometimes for months at a time. We couldn't stay alone, so we came to live with the Tarr family. Dad seemed to trust them. That seemed to be the just right solution.

I sat waiting for dusk. As the sun began to cooperate, I quietly stepped down the stairs to the musty cellar where, among the jars, I would carefully select the "just right size" jar for the capture ahead.

The smell of coal and dampness settled on my senses. I blinked as my eyes adjusted to the dim light. I could see the myriad of jars and bottles on the shelf ahead. There were canning jars and next to them, bottles with long necks and fat necks, jars with brushes crusted over with various half colors of left-over paint.

Someone may have actually cared enough to change the color of a room or a door sill upstairs. It was hard to imagine my foster family finding enjoyment in improving anything. I tried to picture Mr. Tarr laughing and gingerly climbing a ladder to touch up a missed spot above the door sill. This imagining wasn't easy. Mostly what I had seen of him was through the half-closed door of the downstairs bathroom, as he sat in a drunken stupor on the toilet.

I spotted the "just right size" Mason jar with its rusty red lid, counting in my head how many fireflies would fit that space. I hurried up from the cold damp cellar into the coming evening.

The humid air met me like a warm wet sponge. Showers were useless this time of summer, as the humidity kept you feeling like you still needed one. Grey filled the sky, and darkness hovered but had not yet arrived.

I sat and waited. No thoughts, just waiting in the quiet. This was the best part of the firefly fun...just waiting for the first glow. Then there was one, then two, then another and another. I watched as the silky greyness turned to a light charcoal then to a distant darkness. The tiny sparkles multiplied.

What a welcome diversion these little sparkles were from the day life! I'm sure Dad would come rescue us if he knew of the drunken fights and bending over the toilet, waiting for the belt to meet our backsides. Even harder was having to watch the Tarrs sign the guardian line on my report card. We couldn't tell Dad what really went on here. There were no other options. Besides, he trusted them.

I stood up to follow one elusive light only to be distracted by two more quick flashes nearby. Wait until the light goes out, then follow the wings. Catch gently and do no harm.

Catch one, then another, then another. The feel of their brown soft bodies in my fingers demanded gentleness. Handle with care. Lid off, bug in, do no harm. I wondered if these little creatures knew how much they lit up my heart and made me smile. A brief custody… a foster firefly!

I was running now, roaming and carefully snatching with my palm, filling the "just right size" jar. They looked so different in the jar than they did against the night sky. I gazed at my treasure of little town criers with their lamps announcing the coming of night.

They scrambled over one another in their new confinement, lights going off and on at their allotted intervals. A symphony, each instrument sounding at the assigned moment to make their music as one. My jar was lit up. I was done. I sat down and waited…now to just gaze and wonder. Still around me the horizon filled with the uncaptured moving diamonds. I had captured my own gems for a moment.

Suddenly, I heard the call to "Get in here!" That was my signal. We weren't allowed to go inside the house until we were called, and when we were, we better not hesitate!

I wished I were a firefly – to NOT go inside, but to just fly away and light the world.

I opened the lid and, one by one, they crawled over each another. In their haste, they slid downward for each move upward. I tipped the jar sideways and they scrambled to freedom, coming to the edge. Suddenly their wings took over as they realized the open air and safety. Each took leave of the "just right size" jar.

I envied them their freedom, said goodbye and turned to go inside, not yet a firefly.

The Apostate

By Paula Sheller Adams

Freddie jumped through the ceiling of our pond today
and hasn't been seen since.
Stupid Freddie.

'Course, his actions have been strange
And his anatomy seemed rearranged—
two hinged things appeared to trail
on either side of his real tail.
Then we saw two more appear
where you expect to see an ear.

Worst was his mental health of late—
muttering about some different state,
obsessed with the ceiling and swimming 'round it
asking weird questions like what's beyond it.

What's *beyond* it? What really matters is what's on it.
It's where food comes from. Every day.
Free. All we have to do is swim up and eat it
—and be thankful to the Great Tadpole
that gives it to us and loves us.

But no. Freddie wasn't satisfied.
Our ceiling had him hypnotized.
Didn't believe us. Crazy Freddie
talked to the ceiling—said he was ready,

and before we knew it,
Freddie went and hopped right through it.

It was suicide, plain and simple—
just jumped and left without a ripple.
But now, what's even more outrageous

There's a vile rumor that it's contagious

Her First Camel

by Susan Munger

Aysha stretched her thin, bony back for a moment, willing the long, hot day to be over, wishing the wind would stop whining through their stall, wondering if she would ever get enough to eat. As Aysha returned to bending the tiny wires in and around the small golden beads, her father Azam, seated next to her, continued to shape and solder the heavier frame of the next camel.

They sat cross-legged on a thread-bare carpet in a cramped and dim corner of the marketplace, doggedly working their trade from first light to dusk. Every now and then, Aysha would have to pause and hand the camel back to her father for further soldering. No words were exchanged; the rhythm of the work made talk unnecessary.

Aysha's father worked over a tiny fire, using a soldering iron that had a block of copper pointed at the tip to provide just the right amount of heat, uniting the solder to the wire. He knew just how much to apply, having learned this skill from his father before him. Aysha's older brother studied every move and practiced making a stylized camel frame on which the wire and beads would be attached. It was his destiny to someday take over this role while Azam sat home resting and smoking in their scrap of a tent. For his efforts, the son earned a small fee out of the day's take. It wasn't much, but it was more than Aysha got, which was nothing. Nothing, that is, but her meal. Even that was pitiful, but it kept her eight-year-old body sufficiently sustained for another day of work. And another. This had always been the way.

In the market, endless stalls filled numerous alleys full of twists and turns. Smells of cinnamon and curry filled the air, smoke from roasting goat meat wafted across along with the never-ending wind, which was somewhat abated by the stalls themselves and the intricate layout of the market. The market had been in this spot for a thousand years and the town longer than that. Stalls passed from father to son, and the rent for the stall passed from artisan or meat cutter or baker to owner, in addition to a percentage of the days' earnings. An artist like Azam, or a goat butcher or a maker of nan could never earn enough to actually own a stall. They were lucky to earn enough to pay for the vegetables they took home for their evening meal. This had always been the way.

Aysha felt lucky. Although she never got enough to eat [she and her mother always ate after the father and son] she got to come to the market and learn a skill. This was practically unheard of for girls. Most unfortunately, her mother had only the one son, and Azam needed two children to help carry on the work, so at seven years, Aysha had been allowed to join her father and brother and begin her apprenticeship. It would come to nothing, she knew, but still, it brought her to town, to the market, and out of the desert hovel in which they lived.

They rose two hours before dawn when the air was still cool and the wind had died down—Aysha's favorite time of day. They drank a little goat milk with a piece of nan her mother had risen even earlier to bake. Their oven was a hole in the sand covered by a baked clay roof; into the hole went precious pieces of wood which produced a quick, hot fire. Nothing was wasted, for wood—brush, really—was very scarce. The thin flat bread called nan baked quickly. Then they loaded the camel, for which they also had to pay rent. It was a scruffy old beast, but they were used to one another and got on as well as might be expected. They never abused this camel as he was their lifeline to the market, six miles across the bleak, wind-swept desert.

And so in about two hours, the little desert family arrived, parked their camel along with the others, and carried their goods and tools to their stall. Aysha swept it as clean as she could, for it always filled with dirt, sand and debris from day to day. She wanted to make a good appearance for the customers who were mostly tourists from far countries she could not even imagine.

She loved the colors of the market stalls—each merchant vying for attention with golden, purple, green and red cloths draped to provide both shade and eye appeal. Come, they said, Come within and enjoy my shade, and while you're here, take a look at my wares, perhaps buy a little something to take home!

Aysha thought how exciting it would be if someone bought one of her camels. Well, she hadn't actually finished one yet, but she was getting close! She was still learning to arrange the tiny wires and beads just so. They should be spaced perfectly and fill the sturdy framework to make the camel look as real as possible. She knew of course that real camels were not made of golden beads, but she wanted her camels to remind the customers of real camels long after they saw the last one, long after they returned to their far away home where no camels lived.

Out of her reverie, she noticed her father begin to collect his tools and supplies, her brother going to fetch their camel, and she realized the work day was finally coming to an end. Just as Azam was about to pay the stall owner his share, one late customer trotted up to their stall—an older man, overweight, holding onto his straw hat with one hand and waving with his other.

Wait, wait, he called. My wife wants one of your camels!

Azam turned to shoo him away, they were packed up and done for the day; he was tired and wanted to get home to his dinner and his pipe.

Aysha looked down in her hands and was surprised to see she had finished her camel after all.

Her first camel. Silently she offered it to her father, who took it, looked it over carefully and then nodded inquisitively to the customer as if to say This one all right?

The fat man nodded back, extracting money from a worn wallet and, just as inquisitively, looked as if to say Is this enough? The deal was struck. Azam had no energy left to bargain as he normally would, and, besides, the customer offered him far more than he normally charged!

Aysha watched, spellbound, as her camel, her first camel, disappeared into the dust of the market, tucked under the arm of a stranger. She felt a sudden pang, she wanted to call to her camel and say a proper good-bye. But of course that was silly and childish, she knew. There would be many other camels.

Aysha's brother returned with the shaggy rented real camel, loaded up and received his meager coin. Father and son completely ignored the unimportant female. This had always been the way.

The beaded camel now began a journey of some six thousand miles, passing through many hands and not a little time, finally alighting on a card table under another hot sun on another windy day. A sign nearby read Yard Sale: Support Girls' Education.

The eyes of a middle-aged woman went right to the table with the beaded camel; her hands picked it up and caressed it; her heart admired the workmanship and beauty. Hours of intricate work had gone into its creation. She wondered about its provenance, where it had come from, who had made it. But, no matter, she must have it.

How much? she asked with an inquisitive look.

"Trailering"

By Roger G. Ritchey

Did you ever
See a cowed dog
One who gets beaten
Just because...
I saw that today
Renting out an RV space
Only it wasn't any dog
It was the human species
A young girl
Probably 11or 12 years
"Trailering" all of her life
According to her mom
They'd just moved
From Idaho's buck brush
Bent in the body and mind
Two questioning eyes
Peering out of a comely face
Unconsciously begging for help
I just knew...
From a tortured soul
The other two little towheads
Too shy or mentally beaten
To get out of the rusty pickup
Ages 5, 8 and 11 on application
Girl, boy and girl

All sleep together
What can I do?
The 'middle class' is about gone
What can anyone do with
A society that is destroying
One and all?

Cotton-Thread

Gerlinde Schrader

Once upon a time there was a small piece of cotton-thread that couldn't help feeling sorry for himself. He feared that he wasn't important enough the way he was: short and thin. He told himself to make a rope to moor a ship to a dock, but for that he was too weak. For a sweater, he was too short. To connect with other pieces of thread he was way too shy.

"I'm not suited for embroidery either. Alas, I would be too pale and colorless. What if I was silk? I could show off on dresses and fancy gowns. But as it is, I am what I am, a nothing. What can I do? Nobody needs me; nobody likes me. I don't even like myself, not the least bit."

So he talked, the little cotton-thread, to himself. He put on some soft, sad music. He felt so depressed and full of self-pity. He just sat there.

Suddenly there was a knock on the door. It was the little lump of wax. That little lump of wax said to him, "Don't let it wear you down. I have an idea; it just might work."

Cotton-thread said, "Let's put your idea to work. We'll put ourselves together. But wait, for an Easter candle, I am too short to make a wick. And anyway, you don't have enough wax either so that's out. Aha, I think I've got it: let's make a tea-candle. That may work out just right! I believe a small candle would be helpful; much better instead of sitting in the dark to moan and groan. Anything's better than sitting in the dark."

Then the little cotton-thread was so happy. He combined himself together with the tiny lump of wax and said, "Now, my being so short gives a meaning to my existence."

And, you know, maybe there are many short cotton-threads and small lumps of wax out there that could put themselves together and maybe... just maybe...light up the whole world. So don't think a short small cotton-thread is nothing. Just find a small lump of wax and go out into the world and make a difference.

Beets, Plums, Squash and Other Yucky Stuff

By Julie K. Caulfield

Mom tells of the time she got so sick of beets she didn't much care if she ever saw one again. I don't remember the winter she was beaten by the likes of beets, but prone to hyperbole as she is, I'm confident the beet plague didn't last for more than a week or two; that our supper table was graced with at least bread to go with the beets, plums, squash and other yucky stuff. That even at the famine's height, we only lacked meat and milk for a short time.

Beets would grow though, in our inferior soil on the banks of Deer Tail Creek, so I've no doubt there is some element of stretched out truth to her woebegone chronicle of how she came to loathe beets. She was the one that had to plant, weed, harvest, and eventually can the things; she can hate them if she wants.

For my money you could have taken the store-bought canned "Purple Plums" and thrown them into the deepest part of the creek. But, Dad would just buy more. They were the only food-stuff growing up that sometimes caused me to gag in revulsion, and once the gagging reflex was turned on, it was nearly impossible to stop, no matter how hard I tried. I learned to get them down most of the time without gagging because I didn't want Dad yelling at me. However, the disagreeable act of their consumption eventually caused me to become partners in a childish crime of deception with my older brother, Terry, who'd found a way to dispose of unwanted, half chewed foodstuff.

Dad made the money so he got to eat what he wanted. He grew up on chicken, didn't like chicken as an adult, so we never kept chickens for eggs, and seldom had one on the dinner plate. He didn't like pancakes so pancakes were served for suppers when he was away. He wasn't fond of noodles so macaroni or spaghetti or any kind of hot dishes, were out. Milk and cream sauces were not for him. He was a meat and potatoes man, slow to see the depth of shortcomings of his own palette, but had no tolerance for children with food issues. Terry had enormous food issues, and sometimes Dad would force-feed him, making dinner time a miserable, hellish ordeal for all.

Terry had a superior intelligence, it was said, but wasn't smart enough to adapt his survival techniques to simply chew the crap up and swallow it, like I had learned to mostly do. He was too stubborn to compromise any principle—unwanted food or other—and fought Dad tooth and nail.

After a particularly ugly forced-feeding, when the yelling and screaming between our mother and father had simmered down; our mother drew new battle lines. It became apparent the fight now went beyond a parent/child food issue, and into a theater of operation to which only the adults knew the rules. Hence, there reigned an eerie abidance between father and son at the supper table, an audible silence between husband and wife, and a blissful respite for the rest of us. Mom had some secret weapon she was wielding to the nth degree.

One day, a couple of weeks later, it happened to me. I couldn't stop gagging on a single canned purple plum. It would not go down. I imagined I would be force-fed like Terry. Dad bolted out of his chair, but instead grabbing me, he pounded his fist on the table and bellowed, "Just swallow the damn stuff."

Then he stormed out of the house. I guess he never knew how pounding his fist like that on the table in front of me cured the gagging reflex, and that the dreaded purple plum made it all the way to my gut before his boots hit the back door.

Mom picked Jo up out of her high chair, and took her to the kitchen. Peggy and Jane went running off to the living room to play, and that's when Terry showed me his secret. We were underneath our huge round oak dining room table.

"What" I sneered, "are we doing under the table?"

"Well," Terry said dramatically, "haven't you noticed Daddy doesn't force me to eat yucky food anymore?"

"Yes, but I'm sure after that one time Mommy made him stop."

"Mommy got mad alright but that's not what stopped him."

"I think so. It hasn't happened since."

"Haven't you noticed that I actually seem to be eating the yucky food lately?"

It had occurred to me that Terry made it through the last few suppers without a single gagging incident. "So what are you trying to tell me?" I asked, perplexed.

"It goes in here," he said, pointing to the top of a round oak central pillar underneath our table-top. At the bottom of this pillar four huge claw feet jetted out. "It's hollow," he said, grinning like a Cheshire cat.

"Oh, good grief," I gasped.

He demonstrated the hollowness of the central pillar by sticking his hand between the underside of the table and the pillar. The two pieces to our table were secured by four wooden braces, leaving just enough room for a child's naughty hand.

"How?"

"I just knock my fork or spoon off the table when I have a mouthful of food I can't stand to swallow, and ditch it in here while I'm on the floor picking up the silverware.

"What!" I exclaimed.

"Try it the next time we have to eat purple plums."

I did. If spring hadn't come along, and with it an inexplicable urge to do something our mother called "spring house cleaning," we might have indulged in our habit of disposing of yucky food in that hollow center pillar until we'd filled it to the top. I don't remember what we'd imagined we'd do at such a time we'd topped it off, but we were saved from debasing ourselves further because Mom insisted on cleaning the house to an unreasonable degree. Our dumping depot was found out.

One day, after school, she herded us, Peggy too—although she wasn't in on it—under the table and sat us down—hard. She declared that it would happen no more. Her implication was clear as a bell: If you think force-feeding is no picnic, just imagine what it would be like if I told your father about this despicable shenanigans! She pointed and scolded us, and in her inimical way described how gross it was to clean out.

She made us feel lower than worms in the garden, and ended her diatribe with a resounding, "Now grow up!"

I decided I would: That nothing was worth risking a force-feeding. So I swallowed every purple plum served thereafter. Terry choked down the food on his yucky list without dropping silverware to the floor anymore, and to the best of my recollection, the next year Mom's spring cleaning projects went slick as a whistle.

September

By Everett E. Goodwin

September that quintessential season of New England is here.
A marvelous mixture of a season, with its cold/hot, cloudy/
clear weather
And I, I sit between two generations: a great kid of a daughter
and an aging increasingly feisty,
octogenarian mother.
The autumn of life is a yearning, a hope for the future.
That final stretch to the finish seems distant.
The grey stoic winter on its way, warm earth
frozen beneath ice and snow.
Golden brown leaves floating from trees
The rustling of leaves, a warm Indian summer breeze
and
I feel in touch again.

Sometimes I Wish

By Sarah K. Hampton

Sometimes I wish I could draw more than lightning bolts
  and broken hearts,
And that I didn't see those swollen eyes in the mirror.
I wish my thoughts were variables, so I could solve
  for what to say.
Sometimes I wish you could see me in this never-ending
  wall of faces,
Because I see yours so clearly.
Like yellow stars in my midsummer night's sky,
Or the words of a Beatles song,
"I wanna hold your hand."
Well, they were right. I wanna hold your hand,
To hold onto it in the dark when the lights flash in confusion,
And when I choose the wrong door
  to pull me back from my reality.
Sometimes I wonder if you can see the way I look at you,
If you can see the smile
  that's hidden beneath the scars of another.
If you can see what I would give to be special,
What I would give to be that sparkle in your eyes,
What I would give to hold your hand,
And feel my heart beat,
Because I was one of those little white squares
  in the rubix cube of your life.
Sometimes I wish I wasn't that kind of person
  who can write a poem to someone
But can't put together the sounds to say "Hello."

Instead they slip into the cracks of my mouth,
Seeping into my unforgotten regrets.
Sometimes I wish you could see inside my head,
See how the complexity of human touch drives me insane.
And this emotional rollercoaster I'm on,
            trapped in an introvert's nightmare,
Leads me to the iron shackles of a conflicted heart.
You push my buttons like a game controller,
While I try to keep up in this Mariokart race.
You wreck my thoughts with confusion,
But yours is still the first face I see in the crowd.
And sometimes I wish I didn't feel this way
            because it would be so much easier on my own.
Sometimes I wish I didn't see the way you look at her,
But I'm just a friend, stuck in quicksand,
Forced to keep the hurt inside.
And on those days I wish I had a light to give me hope,
Show me I'm not the only person who can't cry
            because it makes me feel weak.

The Miner In Me

by Rosemary Douglas Lombard

for Dave Jarecki

(after Jim Daniel's "You Bring Out the Boring White Guy in Me")

You bring out the miner in me,
the daily blackness of me
red-scrubbed so briefly.

You, my light, bring me the lamp
I strap to my head, the way
I search out our sustenance
from the substance even darker than I.

You bring out the shocks of the drills in me,
their echo through my bones
reechoing through our night
with the rattle of the rails,
the coal that strikes the blackened, beaten cars.
Do they quiver, rattle through your bones?

You, your fear, bring out the fear in me,
eternal fear of falling rock, the fear of eternal silence.

In Work Literary Magazine, 3/26/2012

What the Goose and I Have in Common

By Karen R. Hessen

My conception was a primal spontaneous act of lustful passion that occurred on a night in February, 1947. It took approximately twenty minutes, required no blueprints or special funding and had no preconceived outcome. On the side of masculine inclination it was a rite of marital privilege. On the flip side, it was one of conjugal obligation.

The Goose, however, was conceived after years of strategizing, carefully calculating formulations and detailed preparations. Howard Hughes and steel magnate Henry Kaiser began work in 1942, on a trial airplane to assist moving United States troops and supplies during World War II. The cost of the project surpassed twenty-five million dollars and stretched beyond five years. The war caused a shortage of metal and aluminum, so alternative materials had to be used. The biggest aircraft ever built – six times larger than anything previously flown – was to be made almost entirely of wood.

"It'll never get off the ground, Mr. Hughes," people laughed.

"It'll never fly," they ridiculed.

"Foolhardy."

"It's a 'flying lumberyard'," they said.

In spite of the mocking, Mr. Hughes never gave-up hope.

On November 2, 1947, in Long Beach, California, with Mr. Hughes piloting, the props roared to life, air was sucked under her round belly lifting her wings. The "Spruce Goose" did indeed fly, at an altitude of seventy feet for about one mile. While many of the skeptics and naysayers watched from the ground, Mr. Hughes proved his point.

Ninety-eight miles to the south, in La Jolla, California, another coastal town on the Pacific Ocean, a less historical event was taking place.

"It isn't going to happen, Mr. Brown. She's too big and she's trying to come out backwards, breech – feet first. She just can't be born that way. Sorry, Mr. Brown. Your wife is too small and your baby is too big. It just isn't going to happen like that."

Mr. Brown did not lose hope. Happen it did. On November 2, 1947, after thirty-three hours of difficult labor, while the "Spruce Goose" was making its one and only flight, I did manage my arduous escape, five inches through the birth canal, feet first, into the world. With Dr. J. Blair Pace giving one slap to my round behind, I wailed to life, gulping air into my waiting lungs. After insurance was billed my birth cost $0.17.

"She's too timid," people said.

"Too clumsy."

"She'll never go far."

"Four eyes."

"Don't expect much out of her."

"She's sickly."

"She's too heavy."

"Dull."

While Mr. Hughes kept his "Spruce Goose" in flying condition in a hangar staffed with attendants to meet all of her needs until the early 1980s, I was residing in my own hangar of low expectations.

Unbeknownst to The Goose and me, we both began to extend ourselves at about the same time. I had an opportunity to go back to college, and this time did not listen to the voices that told me I was "lackluster." I tried new things and accepted new challenges. The Goose went on display next to the lovely Queen Mary and for the first time heard people exclaim in wonder at her size and beauty. Unfortunately, she soon also heard the words, "For Sale." Our lives were beginning to change.

In 1992, The Goose, travelling by barge with her wings strapped to her sides, arrived in Portland, Oregon. I, driving a silver 1988 Chevy Corsica with peeling paint and reeling from the effects of an unwanted divorce, arrived by freeway. My arms hung limply from drooping shoulders in a posture of dejection. Both of us faced an uncertain future, lived in temporary housing and sought new friendships.

Soon to be revealed to The Goose was a new destination, a destiny. She was going to be the "main attraction" at the Evergreen Aviation Museum in McMinnville. Choices were made for her. Not for me. I had no destination, no direction, no destiny. I had to live each day, one at a time, seeing what each had to offer, making the best choices of each day's offerings.

While The Goose moved west and settled into life as a museum exhibit, I too moved west. The Goose opened the doors of her fuselage and let visitors walk in. Guests admired the strength of her framework and the beautiful grain of her wooden girth. She heard remarks like: "Incredible," "Amazing," "Magnificent," "Immense," "Phenomenal." She hadn't heard these words since Mr. Hughes spoke them lovingly to her prior to his death in 1976.

I had held onto hope and found my new life in the town of Forest Grove, twenty-eight miles north of The Goose's new home in McMinnville, Oregon. I had made my vulnerabilities visible. I had opened up my heart to love and begun to pour the thoughts and feelings of my soul onto paper. I had found reasons to laugh, given myself permission to cry. I heard my readers comment... "Ahhh," they said, "Lovely," Inspiring," "Rich," "Bold," "Touching," "Delightful," "Colorful."

I recognized myself in Goose's story as I read the museum brochure I held in my hand. It was more than the date – it was the low-expectation and the ultimate overcoming I could relate to – it was the belief and confidence each of our creators had in his creation.

"You know, Goose," I said to her when I visited the exhibit and stuck my head into her massive cockpit. "You need not always be looking up to see someone fly."

On Writing

By Barbara Schultz

I don't remember most of my childhood. All that is left of those early eleven years in Germany are snapshot photos that I go to whenever I open my photo album. I don't feel sad. Most of the time I feel vacant as though I did not actually live there, that I was somewhere else while each morning opened the day and every evening the sunset closed it. The rest is mystery.

I ask my brother Bernd and sister Karin to fill in the pieces, and I am amazed how much they remember in great detail. As I dive into my mind and harvest the smallest scrap of my body-memory, the story emerges and resonates in me. Sadness and an ache in my belly came when I first talked with Bernd, but now there is excitement and sometimes laughter in the tales he recounts.

What is so important about writing that I am willing to open a door so long closed? Maybe it is just that the writer who has entered my life, slinking into the back door with a smile and curiosity, has made her home within me and is excited to weave tiny scraps of memory into something beautiful and important. These memories are in my cell body, and as I write, I trust they will be released. I like the idea that reclaiming cell-body-memory is like having a spring clean where unexpected treasures are found, and all that is no longer of value is released. All that has cluttered up my psychic space will be scattered into the ocean of forgiveness with gratitude.

There were many times when in reflective and tender times, Mum would mention something of her life and our childhood. The snippets of stories told became like the whisper of the wind, a rustle, just the faintest sound that stirred the ears. Then I did not have my inner writer's presence nudging me to listen saying, "This is a note in the story of your life! Listen!"

I don't know when the impulse to write first started. The path from "I might" to action was long and drawn out. First in that nebulous, could or might, the unconscious part of me that thought she do anything and everything, was happy to go along with any new idea. "Oh this is easy, I'll write this in no time, and it's no big deal."

I made the commitment to writing every day.

Apprehensions surfaced. Would I have to change my life in order to write my story? Would I have to learn the skills of writing? Would I have to write and leave the weeds in the garden? Would I have to ask for help from mentors and friends, writers and teachers? Asking for help was not easy for me.

Bang! I hit resistance head on.

"Are you serious? You mean I have to work at this? Writing won't just come all by itself? I only said yes to writing down some memories, I didn't sign on for any more. Now you want to be a writer? You mean actually write more than a few memories? Are you serious? Hang on; I have to take some time to think about this. You have caught me by surprise."

Fear and resistance grew like the genie out of Aladdin's lamp. So many thoughts and fears started bombarding me. They continued with, "Who do you think you are to write this story? You can't remember your childhood," to "What about all the things that you have to do?"

Doing is my passion. Doing is what is acceptable and vital, and doing is my addiction no matter if it is gardening or cleaning or responding to e-mail, getting the volunteers for a Homeless Shelter or Hospice signed up, or working out. Changing that doing habit was like turning a train around on the tracks that was headed in the opposite direction.

My Muse smiled sweetly and gently reminded me, "You have been writing and loving writing for years. Look at all the journals strewn around your home."

"But that is not writing," I blurted.

I made the commitment to writing every day again.

And if I am really honest my muse had been waiting for me for a long time, maybe even forever. She has believed in me and has patiently waited until I was ready. She has loved me, encouraged me and never given up on me. She delights in my presence when I sit and write. She is in the hand that moves my pen and draws from my mind images and words: She is comfortable and determined to wait when the addiction to doing obliterates everything else. She waits for me to come back to writing.

There were days in that early time of writing when paralysis and going vacant were my constant companions. A deep dread seeped into my body and mind, making me feel nauseous from saying yes to something that I no idea how to accomplish. I found myself weepy and vulnerable all day. I learned to trust my body and welcomed each strong feeling knowing that there were emotions held deep inside that needed to become known. Feelings from the past, feelings little me did not know how to deal with all by myself. In welcoming the emotions as fully as I could, I was also being present to a part of me in a loving and caring way.

I noted the resistances that surfaced repeatedly as I started to write. There were times when I suddenly got up out of the chair remembering something that needed my attention right that minute. If I was aware before moving, I breathed into that distraction knowing I could note it in my little to-do book and see to it after my writing time. When I sat to write and nothing came, I continued to wait, committed to that period trusting in the process. I found my addiction to doing was strong and overpowering. To sit and write and let my thoughts wander was torture at times. My Centering Prayer practice of 18 years helped carve out the habit of being with silence.

I persevered and didn't give up, even if there was nothing to show for it day after day. I continued to write every day and kept going as I trusted something would come from my commitment. My friend Susan said that painting for her is so compelling that to not do it would be the hardest thing to do. I want writing to be so compelling that I have to write.

Participate, participate, I will participate in the dream becoming reality. I will love the gift of the Muse as word after word begins to flow onto the page, as images and senses become story and verse. How can I possibly want to stop? I want to be part of the flow of creation.

So I am at the beginning of another adventure, learning another skill, going to classes, sharing time with others who love writing. My support group is there. They will not let me sink into doubt and apathy. I am opening to hidden treasures. Is writing connecting me to a hidden treasure within? Perhaps. And if I really believed this I would write more, would love life more, smile more, have fun, play, rest, be silent, read works that inspire, listen to the music more. I would let my ears hear the pulsating energy in every moment.

I would let my heart shed its fragrance into the world, loving every second of life, every moment as if it's the most wonderful moment of my life.

In that special moment, everything is right, everything is perfect. I love being nudged to dream beyond my imagined abilities.

I will rely on something much deeper and fuller in my writing as I engage with my Muse. I know now she has been waiting patiently, smiling at the delightful dance of moving toward and away, the dance of engaging and resistance. I will remember that my Muse is creating with me.

seeds of singing

by Mary Jane Nordgren

treasure, buried in chest
close under ribcage
etai-eken
of the dani people

willing to die for the future of their people
warriors wounded in ritual battle
bewail mortality but
fear the loss of gem

this inner focus of what matters
protected beyond yam-rich garden
beyond a loved one
beyond fear of dying

held in breadbasket
nourisher of time, of all
one-two-three-many
now, past, forever

protected within self
because it is enduring self
connection with what touches
what feels, what gives meaning

this treasure where all has being
etai-eken—soul
where the being sings

where his life
reaches beyond himself
one with the music of the spheres
etai-eken, his soul
his 'seeds of singing'

Chasing Wonder

By Jessica Page Morrell

My plan was to chase and reclaim wonder. I had it all mapped out—I'd leave behind my feeling-sorry-for-myself-sick bed in the city and return to the mountains and wild places I so loved. I'd unwind next to singing rivers and follow every lonesome bend in the road. I'd camp in remote places, gaze across lakes as the moon shimmered a path on water, and lie out in velvety, high meadows close to the stars and I'd let the magic show overhead melt away all that was sad and hollow and lonely in me.

I've always been a person who needs sky and trees and water to feel still and whole. I've always needed to feel the reverence so necessary for going through daily life; to find the poetry that flows through all things.

But somewhere along the way middle age brought on detours and distractions.

My joints became creakier; my hiking companions fewer; my workload heavier. Instead of camping in the mountains I spent days and months at my computer, my excursions outdoors happened less and less often, my world grew smaller and smaller. After a car accident stranded me indoors recovering for more than a year, I knew I needed to reclaim the part of me that is most alive and most reverent, because a soul sickness had set in.

I began by walking at dusk in local parks and bike trails, taking in the dewy finery of springtime, marveling in the soft, perfumed air, reclaiming something dormant within me. As summer came on, I was stoked for the marvels of rare bird sightings, brilliant night skies, and trees that whispered our campsite to sleep while the last embers of the campfire died out.

Of course when a person seeks wonderment in wild places, often fate has other lessons to bestow.

Our first excursion was to a mountain lake in the Cascades. I was with my daughter, granddaughters and son-in law and we arrived the second week of July under a steady mist, cooked dinner under a downpour, and I fell asleep with the sound of rain drumming on my tent roof. And woke just after dawn in a puddle, every inch of me wet and cold. Crawling out of the tent, my breath visible in the mountain air, the campground was drowning–about sixty gallons of water ballooning the tarps hanging over the table, a foot of water in the fire pit, wet everywhere, a steady dripping from the sky and trees.

I changed and added layers of clothes in my car and set to work starting a fire. And I did manage to build one after bailing out the fire pit with a tin cup and procuring dry kindling and wood from my car's trunk. My granddaughters woke as the fire was going, we crowded near it for warmth and I taught them old Girl Scout songs and "Here Comes the Sun" as they drank hot cocoa and I my Earl Grey. And layers of time and memory settled in around us, huddled under the dripping trees.

When I drove back down the mountain a few days later I stopped at the first Fred Meyer's store to return the off-brand tent that had allowed water to leak in through the zipper. I must have looked slightly mad with my filthy nails, wild hair, and clothes lumpy from sleeping in them damp, clutching a bottle of red wine that I planned to drink later with dinner after a scalding shower.

Our next campground was nearby on the Clackamas River, a pure, noisy river I've come to love as it winds and scours its way through steep-walled canyons, mountains, and forests, to finally join the Willamette. As long ago as 10,000 years Native Americans lived, fished and hunted along the river and built villages, the river named after one of these tribes. Later, most of these people disappeared, wiped out by epidemics, then surrendering their lands. But the river still tells their stories.

The trees at the campground were tall and the whole place smelled sweet like cedars and ferns. That first night I staked out a place to lie in the grass and watch the stars. But it was a Friday night and the open meadow thronged with giddy, loud teenagers. Some obviously stoned or drunk, some tamping down a wildness that seemed about to explode, "Dude, like we're going to be in soooo much trouble." The following nights the clouds were ominous with thunderheads, or I was asleep before the stars rose to shimmer in full regalia. But still I expected nature to heal and move me, and each hike to heal and move me, and each hike around a lake or sudden view of Mt. Hood after the morning clouds broke way brought me closer to, well, me.

Then we traveled south to a popular campground on a popular lake in the middle of the state. I hated everything about it—the closeness of the campsites, the lack of old trees to shelter under, the noise of dogs and campers too close by. As dusk fell, a few sites down, campers were projecting Mall Cop on an outdoor screen. Wonder never seemed more elusive.

I forgot to mention the heat. The temperatures were in the high 90s and as rarely happens here in Oregon, that first night it didn't cool down and I sprawled on top of my sleeping bag poaching in my own sweat. Morning dawned in a blaze of copper. By noon temperatures had climbed beyond 100. We spent the day in the lake or under a nearby canopy, trying to outsmart the sun.

When we returned from the lake later in the day, drained and cranky from the heat, neighbors had moved into the site next door. They had shifted around the picnic table so that it encroached on our site, they owned a dog that barked at us every time we moved, and that night, as I was again tossing miserably in the heat, two men merely feet from my tent farted and laughed and chatted, as I gritted my teeth at every word and explosion.

The second day I contracted a stomach ailment and made dozens of trips to the bathroom. When you scurry to the bathroom that often, you recognize the campsites around you, especially the group camped right next to the facility, playing cards, sun dappling onto their table their laughter echoing in the trees.

Late in the afternoon, skin taut from heat, I drove my granddaughters to a shower in the campground, the air conditioning blasting in my car. The small building baked in the blistering sun was steamy and two women were bathing children in adjacent shower stalls. One of the women, who I judged to be in her sixties by her voice, was cooing to a toddler, her voice as soothing as a lullaby. "What a big boy you are," she praised, then reassured, "all done," praising him all the while.

Eavesdropping as I helped six-year-old Paige negotiate shampooing, drying and clean underwear, I realized that the child was not hers. That she was helping out a stranger, a mother of two toddlers. In those moments of soft mother's voices and children's sweet murmurs, in the steam and spray of water, and the smells of baby powder, it was as if time had stopped. Then they emerged from their showers, a girl about 18 months and a boy of about three, both shy, and pink and damp. And there was a stillness in the room, as the children eyed my older girls, grace wafting in the steam.

We headed back to our campsite, towels wrapped around our heads like turbans. I felt so becalmed it was as if I'd received a blessing. And it came to me that wonder isn't always a sky show or the sunset washing plumes of color across the summer Pacific. It also arrives in small moments of kindness and comfort. And wonder of wonders, later that night the stars were dazzling and seemed so close you could ride away on one up and up reaching far galaxies.

The Boat

By Nel Rand

Snow was falling from a slate gray sky when Sara arrived at the lake and parked in front of the weathered cabin. It was late afternoon Christmas Eve. She was losing the light.

The boat had been on her mind all day. She had built the boat here. Years ago, with her father, when her skin was smooth and the color of fresh peaches, and she ran everywhere instead of walked.

The boat was the vessel that held the Holy Eucharist of her youth, her happiest memories. That's what called her back to spend the holidays here at the lake. Her daughter had tried to talk her out of going alone but Sara knew where she needed to be.

The family had vacationed here in the summers, and once, Sara remembered, for Christmas. It was snowing then, like today, and she and her brother Mike had built a snowman.

They had carried in logs from the shed and built a blazing fire in the wood-stove. Mother baked cinnamon rolls from scratch, and they all sang old Norse carols that Mother played in minor keys on her silver flute.

Sara looked back at the full-to-the brim box of wrapped Christmas presents given to her by her daughter and two grandchildren, with a promise from her not to open them until Christmas morning. She had all the makings of a Christmas dinner, including cinnamon rolls for breakfast, if she had an appetite and her energy held out.

Bundles of pressed logs and plenty of matches, candles, and several kerosene lamps were perched on the back seat of the car.

She shivered and got out of the car to stretch her legs and crunch through the snow that now covered the ankles of her boots.

Through the thickening veil of snow, the empty woodshed looked lonely. No one came to the cabin anymore, not since Mother, Father, and Mike had died. Her nuclear family; they were all gone. Her husband had died ten years ago, and her daughter's family preferred vacationing in more sunny climes.

Unpacking would have to wait. A longing that made her heart beat faster led her to the back yard shed where the boat lived, alone and stiff with old age. As she pulled off the raggedy blue tarp the irrefutable memories of childhood captured the winter's air and turned it to a summer's wine.

The boat was simple in design. She loved it. It was the one thing she and her father had made together.

The boat looked smaller than she remembered. Some of the boards were rotting, but she managed to get it horizontal and pull it out by the frayed rope attached to the bow. She dragged it down to the lake, careful not to slip and fall.

It was getting colder and a layer of ice was forming under the powdery top snow.

Nudging the boat out onto the frozen lake, she scooted inside from a sitting position and picked up the crude oars she and Father had carved, pretending to paddle.

She lost herself in summers past, when she had been intimate friends with families of beaver, knew all the deep holes where the trout hung out, sat in silent wonder with red-tailed hawks.

"Sara girl, you live in that boat. Why don't you come off the lake and visit with us. We have such precious little time here together." She recalled her mother's frequent plea. "No regrets," she said to the approaching night as she stuck out her tongue to catch snowflakes.

Seeds of...

Section IV
– Remembering

The Big Wind

by Susan K. Field

Whoosh! The brass lamp flickered twice. Then it went dark. Our window panes rattled with a fury as fierce as Sister Marion's raging ruler in my second grade classroom. Looking outside, I sat on the edge of the couch with my arms hugging my knees so tight they ached. Another thunderous clap of wind whipped our aluminum screen door back and forth, back and forth until the invisible beast ripped the door off its hinges, propelling the mangled frame into the rhododendron bushes. Dad and Ed, our neighbor, ran around our Maple tree. The thick trunk I had sat beside during summer picnics of Coca-Cola and potato chips now lay on its side. Branches stretched over the sidewalk and blocked the street. Dirt clung to the exposed root ball that stood about my eight-year-old height.

The men carried their axes and then started to chop at the trunk because cars coming down our street couldn't get around it. Tails of Dad's plaid shirt slapped his lean body and leaped around as if skipping rope. At one point, Dad held onto the tree, bracing himself against another onslaught of heavy wind— wind so forceful it pushed Ed sideways.

"Oh no," I gasped, gulping in a mouthful of air. Now Ed's fir tree tumbled over too, right where he had been standing. And, I realized, if that gust hadn't tossed him aside, the tree would have crushed him.

Within minutes, more trees cracked, split and crashed to the ground. Imagining I were a bird flying above the scene, the street looked like pick-up sticks on my bedroom floor after letting them scatter from my grasp. As I sat alone in our dim Portland bungalow, I wondered, 'Is this the end of the world?' Growing up in Oregon, I knew rain and snow, but not hurricanes.

A hollow feeling quivered through me. Even though I promised Mommy that I'd never bite my fingernails again, I started back up. The cuticles puffed with fresh pink chew marks. I worried about Dad out there in that chaos of swirling debris. And, I fretted about Mommy. She was out there, too—somewhere. So, I folded my hands, closed my eyes and whispered a prayer.

"God. I know you do miracles. Please make a miracle. Let our world live."

Soon, Dad hurried inside. "Let's go get Mum!" he yelled. "We can't let her walk home alone in this."

Springing to my feet, I obeyed his order. Although, I had a million questions, like, 'Is Mom okay? What's happening? Are we going to die? How are we going to get her? The car's in the garage and the tree's in our way.' But, I didn't ask. This was no time to ask. No, not a good time at all to probe him with my school-girl questions. Even if I had asked Dad, he couldn't have heard me because the ravenous wind ate our words and buried them under our fear. He bundled me in my red car coat and we set out walking. I clung to him. And, secretly, I think he clung to me.

Our house was three blocks away from the stop where mommy got off the Rose City Transit Company bus every day after work. At the intersection of our street were a grocery market and a mobile home dealership. We walked only as far as a few houses and my legs already felt tired from straining against that powerful wind. Garbage sailed in the currents.

Branches blew by us. My mind screamed. 'I wanna go home. I'm scared!' But, I told my thoughts to hush. I had to be brave and keep up with Dad.

As we approached the bus stop, I stretched my neck forward to see Mom. She wasn't there. My heart sank.

"Oh, Mommy. Where are you?"

A moment later, the wind shifted and flowed away like an ocean's gentle tide. The calm eased my fright and let me breathe again. Then, as if Satan himself exploded from the hell the nuns were always telling us about, a blast as loud as Dad's hunting rifle belched out. Metal cracked and popped. The devil pried sheet metal from the trailers and flung the whirling pieces like guillotine blades straight toward us.

"Get down!" Dad pushed me to the ground and covered my body with his. The weapons sliced through the air just above our heads. Lying flat and motionless, we stayed until a lull in the storm allowed us to run and crouch near the market's front door. Finally, two hours later, Mom's bus came.

"Mommy! Mommy!" I cried, running to her as she stepped off the bus.

"It's alright, honey. It's going to be alright," she said and smoothed my flying hair down. "Now, let's get home quick."

The three of us huddled together and zigzagged our way around fallen trees, upside down lawn chairs, tin cans, roof shingles and newspapers until we reached home.

Later, Ed and his wife came over to eat with us. The whole house was dark, save for the blue flames of our camp stove and the light from the Coleman lantern. The grown-ups talked. Dad told the story of our walk in the big wind. Their stories weaved in and out of my dozing slumber. My eyes popped open when I heard Ed's wife proclaim in her thick Southern accent, "My goodness. It was a miracle you all made it through that hurricane." She paused and drank her coffee. "Just a miracle."

'Yes,' I thought and roused as Mom served us a dinner of canned tangy Franco-American spaghetti and sweet, delicious hot cocoa. Both soothed my gnawing stomach. But, nothing, no, nothing that night tasted sweeter than the miracle.

My Father's Store

Brooklyn 1957

By D. K. Lubarsky

Wind and snow dance on concrete streets,
Slicing through city canyons of pre-war brick,
Tattooed with casement windows and iron laced fire escapes
This day, like all the others, shortened by winter's darkness

My father's hardware store smells like the kerosene
He keeps in the back room
I cut kitchen shades to measure
        with confidence born of youth,
And likewise keys proportioned to locks

I am too young to carry 12 foot rolls of linoleum
The way father does, on his back, up six flights of stairs
But I help out each Saturday in the weeks before Christmas,
Selling white china cups and bright red Christmas tree stands

The smell of kerosene, and the taste of piping hot bagels
Still brings me back to those days
Munching hot bagels on the ride home,
In the days before the anger.

Eyes of an Angel

By Rebecca Robinson

We were not allowed
more than an index finger of bath water
To leave lights unattended
waste food
enjoy a Coca-Cola, without splitting it with Daddy

Yet not a word was spoken
when our Depression-age parents
commissioned an art piece
for our modest home

A gifted hand resurrected you…warm again
facing the sun
that beamed through wedding dress chiffon curtains
in Mama and Daddy's bedroom window

Your portrait, perfect in soft pink
pinned against a heaven-blue wall
The crucifix kept you company
Jesus, above the light switch
pointing at you
weeping
cracked Palm Sunday leaves
to catch His tears

A voyeur
I fixed my eyes on that dusty glass
wished you alive

Your dark chocolate eyes
save my life
encourage me along
a dim, starlit path
show me the way
to God

banister to wisdom

By Mary Jane Nordgren

at the head of the flight
of the steep stairs
i climb up and on
my right foot dangling
fifteen feet over narrow
hallway below

i close my eyes
afraid, but determined
i've seen my uncles
and my older sister do this
but i wouldn't try
when they could watch

my palms are slippery
as i try to grip
the dark, polished wood
slowly i ease my near-prehensile
toes from around the decorative
uprights and let
my bum first begin to move

i lift left foot
from its final anchor
and the slide begins in earnest
balled red-plaid dress and
white cotton panties against
the lacquered railing

i clutch at, but cannot grasp
the smooth, wide rail

i swoosh
faster and faster
gritting my baby teeth
to keep from screaming

a gasp escapes my mouth
as i descend, but grandma
doesn't hear me until
i've reached round, decorative end curl
swished near-sideways off it
and clattered to the wooden floor

i'm not crying, exactly
momma would have
rushed to pick me up
and coo sweet assurances
but grandma, mother of
three boys, stands arms akimbo

come over here, and I'll
pick you up, she says
I'd come to you but I have
a bone in my leg

i stagger up, blinking, and
check that i'm okay

next time, don't come down so fast
she says over her shoulder
as she returns to the kitchen

i feel so bad about that bone in her leg
i hold onto the banister as i look back
up its length; so much to learn

(first published in Frail the Bridge)

Down on the Farm

By Lois Akerson

"MmmMornin' Elsie", mooed Bessie, the cow, stifling a yawn. "I didn't get much sleep last night. I think the water temp in my waterbed was too cold. I'm afraid my milk production rate will be down today."

"I know what you mean", Elsie replied, "I couldn't get to sleep either last night because those young heifers wouldn't turn down the volume on the HDTV."

Fantasy? Maybe not. Iowa farmer, Kirk Christie, reports that his contented cows put out an extra 10 percent of milk after lounging on their waterbeds near the flat-screen TV he's given them. But if waterbeds for the entire herd don't fit your budget, a study by Newcastle School of Agriculture in Great Britain says that a "more personal touch" can be achieved without spending any money. Farmers saw higher milk production by personalized pampering and calling their cows by name.

We called our cows by name when I was growing up on the farm in Bloomfield, Nebraska many years ago. One tall, pure white cow we called Snowball. She was the one that my big brother, Martin, chose for my first milking lesson. I sat alongside Snowball on a three-legged milking stool, with a huge, shiny, silver bucket between my legs.

"Pay attention," Martin said. "You start with your index finger gradually closing your palm. Then your middle finger, ring finger and pinkie in a simultaneous motion, forcing the milk downward out of the teat. The first few squirts are loud and tinny-sounding until the bottom of the bucket covers with milk and the squirt sound changes to a slurp, slurp rhythm. Go ahead, try it."

Hesitantly, I tried it but Snowball realized she was being touched by an amateur. She swished her dirty, stringy tail into my face, turned her head, looked me straight in the eye and kicked, knocking me off the milking stool and spilling the milk all over me.

"Darn you, Snowball," I yelled. "Just look at what you've done!"

"Moooaaahhh" was her only reply.

Martin finished the milking and then went to check his trap line. Moles, gophers and other rodents would burrow underneath the planted crops in the field, doing considerable damage to them and consequently to the expected harvests. Dad gave Martin 25 cents for each one that he caught. This particular day, Martin caught more than he anticipated. A large black animal with a white stripe down his back had his front foot caught in a trap. Instead of being grateful when released, the animal turned his back to Martin ejecting an excruciating spray possessing a strong, noxious odor.

With his eyes burning and his sinuses seared, Martin headed for home. When he got to the back door, Mom took his clothes and put them in the burn barrel, gave him a bar of lye soap and told him to wash off in the horse trough. Dad, angered because the horses couldn't drink the soapy water and overwhelmed by the stinking smell, told Martin he'd have to sleep in the barn that night.

Our family lived in a two-story farmhouse at the end of a dirt road. Our bedrooms were upstairs which were so hot and humid in the summer that sleep was impossible, but in winter we had to bury ourselves under quilts to keep warm.

My older sister, Ruby, and I shared a bedroom. Tall, with big brown eyes, Ruby was always curling and fixing her beautiful, brown hair. Puzzled as to why she would lie down on the floor before bedtime and exercise. I asked, "Ruby, why do you do all that stuff?"

"Well, she replied, "I have to keep my body curvaceous so someone will ask me out for a date." And that's just what happened the next Saturday night.

Jim was to pick her up at 7:00 and she felt sure that would give her plenty of time to get ready. She was so excited and wanted to look just right! She heated water on the kitchen woodstove and poured it into the big, round metal bathtub. She was about to step into the tub when she heard a knock at the back door. The window shades were up, leaving her silhouette in plain view. Painfully embarrassed, she grabbed her towel and made a hasty retreat.

One Sunday, our family piled into our Model "A" Ford and headed for church. The air was murky and humid and on the way home Dad kept looking at the dark and menacing clouds. Dreaded anticipation permeated each of us when we got home. Dad's face was serious as he yelled, "All of you, into the storm cellar! Now!"

"But, Dad, can I go get Ralphie first?" Martin asked.

"Never mind that flea-bitten dog. Just get yourself down into the storm cellar! Anna, go get a loaf of bread and a butcher knife; and bring some water too. Martin, fill the kerosene lantern and, Paul, go get the axe in case we need it."

We crowded into the cellar and then Dad closed the door. And then it happened! The roar and howling of the approaching tornado filled us all with gut-wrenching fear. We heard unknown objects crashing around us. We clung to one another, hoping that the storm would soon be over.

Then, all of a sudden, silence.

Dad tried the cellar door again and again but couldn't open it. Then taking the axe, he cut through the door and we climbed out. The sight that greeted us was devastating; sticks of lumber; tree branches and debris everywhere; chickens clucking excitingly; feathers in the air; chicken house flattened.

But then Dad smiled and started hugging us saying, "Thank God, we're all safe!"

And that included Ralphie who jumped up and greeted my brother excitedly.

A smile lights up my face as I recall these unforgettable memories and I realize how lucky I am to have grown up on the farm in Bloomfield, Nebraska.

Young Father Time

By Roger G. Ritchey

Do you remember your first watch? I'm guessing I was probably eleven years old when I managed to save enough moolah from picking strawberries and that telling or knowing the time was important enough to me to part with a couple of 1950's dollars. Telling time with your stomach wasn't going to cut it, because at ten or twelve snot-nosed years, hunger pains are a constant. And with the Sun for your clock you always have to be subtracting or adding minutes depending on if it was summer and dust time or winter and mud time.

My first time piece was a so called pocket-watch simply because that's where you kept it. All male pants then had this small pocket designed to hold the watch on the right hand side just above where the big deep knife and gum pocket was located. Dad wore blue bib work overalls and they had a nice safe place too. And older men like my Dad or Grandpa had a vest as part of their Sunday getup so the watch was usually kept there.

Originally my first watches were referred to as a dollar watch because that is what they cost for many years with production starting amazingly in 1892 by Ingersoll/Rand according to my wife's computer. And, lucky me, I caught the watch after early nineteen fifties inflation banged on in, making me spend two bucks. Sometimes this 'fine piece' was called a potato-watch and I never knew why. Maybe Ireland was into trading spuds for watches then.

All of these watches had a big fat stem for regular winding but some had trouble going the full twenty-four hours and others hung on for maybe thirty hours. This is where the saying came from, "A real stem-winder." Winding was naturally an everyday affair and you could look rather intelligent doing it if you got that certain Socrates cast to your farm boy face. And if you put the watch up close to your ear, its ticking was quite audible for young virgin ears.

The other notable thing about these time tellers was that if you got twelve months of 'life,' count yourself super lucky. Someone in this industry had discovered built-in obsolescence, but of course the watches got a lot of banging around and probably wet, too, especially if your home place had two creeks on it like ours. Us kids used narrow and shallow Carpenter Creek for wading or floating our little homemade boats and Gales Creek for swimming, but that and the girls spying on us sometimes Summer naked boys is another story.

Anyways if you took one of those 'fine Bulivas' apart it was obvious water seals cost too much. One guy I know got upset when his time piece quit after just a few weeks of proud ownership and he heaved it towards a shed. A couple, three things happened then, first his dad found it and got upset which wrangled his mom into the deal with both of them coming down hard on the kid. But it turned out good, 'cause hitting the shed wall made both the front and back pop off and so when the kid put them back on the watch started keeping time—after a fashion.

It was somehow always enjoyable for me to watch my dad remove his silver-cased watch from his pocket and peer at the time. This well-worn watch had a leather thong attached to it and the other end sometimes hooked to a metal button.

My Grandpa Mac's pocket watch was gold and may have been a retirement watch; it had a small gold chain probably six inches long for attaching in case you got tipped upside down. And if it wasn't a retirement gift it should have been, 'cause most work weeks were six days then; with the days lasting for twelve hours, plus retirement age was seventy. There were a lot of guys who never hung on that long.

Then I next remember some kid coming to school with a Mickey Mouse watch strapped to their wrist—and weren't they puffed-up proud. I never had one and always thought they looked kinda dumb, but maybe that was just kid jealously talking. I do think all of the Mouse watches were worn by town kids and they just didn't look like they could stand up to milking cows and shoveling shit.

Anyways, pocket watches and the Mickey Mouse Jobbies hung around until decent wrist watches came down the pike. Now of course if you are an Oil Sheik, Movie Star or Stud Athlete you can spend several thousand dollars and one can get a watch that has so many dials or knobs that it make your head swim. And that's the way it was, well, mostly, I think.

December 8, 1941, and the Uchiyama Family

By Muriel Marble

It was a dreary, wet Monday morning as I rushed off to catch the school bus for the forty minute ride to Forest Grove High School. We had no radio and probably no electricity yet in our rural home. Sunday had been a normal, quiet day. As I entered the bus, my life changed. Everyone was talking about the news from the previous day: Pearl Harbor had been bombed! We did not know how to believe this, but knew it had to be true. Our lack of radio had given my family one more war-free day than my classmates had.

As we entered school, we were directed into the auditorium rather than to our classrooms. I was with my good friend Lea Uchiyama, who was a grade ahead of me. On the stage was a large radio with a loudspeaker. The principal called us to attention. I do not remember if we started with the salute to the flag, but we probably did. The radio was turned on, and President Franklin Roosevelt started speaking. He told us of the bombing at Pearl Harbor the previous day. He announced that we were declaring war on Japan as he was speaking. My next memory is of filing out of the room and walking toward our first period class. As I walked with Lea, I said, "I am sorry for you."

"Why?" she replied. "I am an American."

I knew she was referring to her birth here, which gave her citizenship, as contrasted to her parents, denied citizenship and even the ability to own land. Their farm was purchased in the name of her eldest brother John, also born here. The family was hard working, responsible, and respected in the neighborhood. Their strawberry fields were the first in the community, providing income for neighbors who picked the fruit in the worst of the Depression. We walked on to class, to lives forever changed.

By May, 1942, fear had caused the Japanese to be restricted to their homes after 8:00 PM. I distinctly remember being called to the school office where I was given Lea's graduation diploma to take to her. She was not allowed to attend her ceremony. It was after the curfew.

Hard work had produced a good crop of berries, but the family was not allowed to harvest them. Instead the Uchiyamas were ordered to the Portland International Livestock Exposition quarters, which had been cleaned out for holding areas for all the Japanese families in the Portland area. They were given a choice of a camp away from the coast, or to be resettled in eastern Oregon and put to work in the fields near Ontario. Lea's father chose the latter. I was fifteen, and the outrage I felt over the injustice still brings tears to my eyes. Until then, I had trusted the government. Nevermore.

We had friends who favored Germany and the German Bund. They were not affected. Unfair, unfair, unfair! In the fall of 1943, I was assigned to write a 3000-word paper for my college English class. I chose to write about the Japanese relocation. The only information I could find was in the locked areas of the big downtown library in Portland. How I wish I could find that paper. It was lost during moves later on.

Mom wrote to Lea, urging her to not let anger destroy her. Lea to this day remembers that letter and how it helped her.

Lea's brothers and sisters all graduated from college. Her brothers all became either dentists or doctors of medicine, settling in Ohio and the Midwest. Lea studied to be a nurse in Washington, D.C. She tells how, when she was exhausted during training, she remembered the berry field and kept going. She was NOT returning to the fields. She married a dental surgeon, and they have a lovely home in Dayton, Ohio, coincidentally two miles from where my grandmother was born. When she found this out, she discovered much of my family history. One year I stayed with her a few days while we researched my genealogy.

One year in the late eighties the Uchiyama family was having a reunion in Seattle for a family wedding. Lea and I made plans, and I hosted an outdoor reunion on the hillside where I had grown up. I had a notice put into the Forest Grove News Times. The Fern Hill neighbors all came to voice the regrets no one had had a chance to say. Tributes were given to the hard work and the impact the family had had on the community. All seven of the Uchiyama children were there. The veteran classmates who had fought the Japanese in World War II were especially there. Even Willford Kalsch, the teacher of our one-room grade school, was able to attend. It was a simple pot luck picnic and contrasted with the fancy dinners these professional people were accustomed to. It was just right. God blessed us with perfect weather and good down-home food. It was a healing time for all of us as we looked out over the lovely Tualatin Valley and remembered so much.

Nine Panes of Glass

by Rebecca Robinson

Both black and white memories
and kaleidoscopes of color
Children in rubber boots
slick rain jackets
Giggling schoolgirls smacking bubblegum
Tree branches dance high as
giant choir members in Hallelujah applause
Leaves flicker into shiny coins
Ducks move in a prow and disappear
surrounded by pine and oak trees
Glistening raven lands atop a Christmas tree
and strikes the pose of a dark angel
Technology lurks within and without
Cranes blush among skim milk daylight
Canadian geese overlook a drizzly gray day
and find peace that plumps their wings
Take the time today
when it's not raining
for God's hearty laugh
as it forms ripples on the pond
and fly away

Beach Dog Café

By Eva Foster

The gray sky of the storms had cut off my view from the railing. The rain kept me from sitting outside.There was no sun to warm me.creativity was on its last ember. The October storms I had come to watch and inspire me held me prisoner.

Starbucks was eight miles down the road.I gathered up my book, Writing Down the Bones, and decided to take a few bills, my debit card and my keys. After all, this book on writing was exalting the importance of spontaneity!I was determined to exercise that and travel light.I navigated the long stairway to the parking lot and tucked everything away in my pockets. Opening the car door, I thought ahead to the delightful caramel mocha and small breakfast sandwich awaiting me.

The constant companion of ocean view on my left drew me in. As I drove past the smorgasbord of shops, I had a yearning for something unfamiliar.slowing down through Depoe Bay I headed toward the Lincoln City Starbucks. This end of town or the other?The landscape of small buildings seemed to blend together and I thought I had whizzed past my destination.My eyes jotted from sign to sign.Then I spotted a familiar unfamiliar.I had seen the sign before, but had always assumed it was closed.The large blue letters within purple squiggly vines read "BEACH DOG CAFÉ." I did that moment of spontaneity, gave in to my indulgence, and told myself to stop.The gravel spun as I turned around and headed for the parking lot.It was half full but the lights at the window seemed welcoming and I could see faces inside.

"Hello and welcome to Beach Dog Café," came a voice greeting me even before I had shut the door. Framed dog pictures were everywhere.Had they been wallpaper, it would have been a monstrous stripping job.

"Someone sure loves dogs," I said to the unknown voice.

"Not as much us as our patrons.Most of these are their pictures." A young man guided me to a small table in a quiet corner."Just one this morning?"

"Yes"

My eyes took in the framed photos.Big dogs, little dogs, red dogs, white dogs, spotted dogs, smiling dogs.I looked for a familiar breed. There she was, a yellow Labrador: our Annie looking back at me.

"Our dog died about a year ago. I still miss her." I said, to begin the conversation.

"That's really hard, isn't it?" said the waiter, handing me a menu. A wave of compassion came to his eyes and then it was replaced by an inviting smile."Coffee?"

Fully intending not to have a big breakfast, I ignored my intentions, dove in, and ordered the largest omelet on the menu. The taste and fragrance of fresh coffee settled me. I opened my book and dove back into the chapter on becoming part of my surroundings. I knew for sure if I became part of these surroundings, I would wag my imaginary tail and give out an approving "WOOF."

Then came the waiter with THE plate: a perfectly light omelet filled with pepper jack and smothered with lightly fried onions, baby spinach, cilantro and tomatoes. The greens and yellows and browns with a dash of red would have pleased any artist's palette, but the only palate I cared about at the moment was the one inside my mouth. Laying serenely beside the omelet were evenly- sliced, half-dollar sized, well-browned potato slices, and lots of them. At two o'clock sat one small quarter of a grapefruit slice and one lonely grape.Perfect presentation.

I consciously pulled out my book and began to read and eat. After a couple of pages, I rewarded myself with a bite of omelet and a few potato slices. The fresh spinach and cilantro dangled mischievously on the tines of my fork.Mmmmmm... reading had never tasted so good!

As I read, I took note of the suggestions on the familiar and the unfamiliar. I continued devouring book and breakfast and gave myself over to becoming "one with my surroundings." The light egg omelet suddenly became a cape of delight around my shoulders, and the small baby spinach leaves and feathery cilantro became flags in my hands. I set the greens down to catch one of the potatoes rolling toward me like a giant tire and quickly devoured it.

"More coffee?" interrupted my thoughts. This time it was a pleasant middle aged woman with a lovely smile.

"Yes, thank you. This breakfast is pure delight," I blurted. "First time I've been here. I almost missed your little café. So glad I turned around."

"So glad you came in. Enjoy your meal."

I continued with my reading. Good timing. From a page of my book, a quote leapt at me; the words of Kalagiri Roshi, "It is very deep to have a cup of tea."

I wished I had my notebook to write this down, but then I realized this was not a note-taking kind of moment. I was experiencing the very deep.

As I looked up from my reading, the "NO DEBIT CARDS, NO CREDIT" sign caught my attention, strategically placed between the hounds and the cock-a-poos. The sign had greeted me at the door but I had missed it.

I reached into my pocket feeling the few bills and debit card within.Embarrassed, I peered at my empty plate.

I flagged down the waiter.

"I don't know how I missed the signs.I don't believe I have enough cash to pay for my breakfast.I only have a debit card and a few small bills."

"There is an ATM next door. We'll be around until 2:30 today. Drop it off later if you can. If not, it's no problem" Filling my cup again, he went on to the next table.

I looked up at the flop-eared dachshund staring down at me."Yup" he said."You're off the hook!"

The total on my receipt was fifteen dollars even.I dug into my left pocket and found two fives. I fished again and found a dollar in my right pocket. I started to close my book, when I spotted a bill holding a place in chapter seven. It was a five. I made it with a dollar to spare.

I relaxed, sipped my coffee and finished my breakfast guilt free.My book and I headed for the register.

"I found enough cash after all."I apologized for the dollar tip and oozed gratitude for the pleasantness of the past two hours.

"You are quite welcome." He smiled. "Hope we see you again."

"I'll be back," I said.I knew I wouldn't leave town tomorrow morning without returning for another cup of java.I gave a quick backward glance, taking in the aromas and the surroundings. I paused and thanked the dogs too, with a surefire "WOOF" under my breath, as the door closed behind me.

A Trip Through the Heartland

By Sandra Mason

In 1987 I applied for a fellowship in Oregon and embarked upon my first sabbatical, returning to my home state from my time amid the alien corn in New York. A year's absence from my residence required considerable planning. My sister knew my vulnerability: I was newly-divorced and had just survived a struggle with the silent enemy, endometriosis. She decided, with her teen-age daughter, to fly to New York to help me ready the house, and then we would all drive together cross country back to Oregon—a grand adventure.

Linda was indispensable help. We got all my extra belongings into boxes in the basement and made a diagram of how we would load the car, with baggage for three passengers along with everything I would need for a year, including my large computer monitor, printer, and books. Oh, and the two cats in their carriers, and their litter box. With Linda and me in the front seats, Nancy and the cats in the back seats, and the hatchback arranged like a Chinese puzzle, we were ready.

My family has always been economical and efficient—an early version of multi-tasking. We had been assigned to check in on relatives scattered across the country. Our first stop was to be Des Moines, Iowa.

We remembered Uncle Verlan from his visits to Oregon in the '50s. Verlan was about 5'3" tall—in fact, his nickname was Shorty. He had married a tall, stylish woman named Ruth, who resembled Natasha from "Rocky and Bullwinkle."

Ruth had dark hair, was slim, smoked cigarettes and drank highballs, and wore Elizabeth Arden Victory Red lipstick. Together they looked like Mutt and Jeff—tall and short—but they were childless bon vivants. We recalled their turns around our living room as if it were a dance floor—they had seemed so grand and gay.

By the late '80s Ruth had succumbed to lung cancer and Verlan had gone bald. Now he was retired and living in his own small house with a woman thirty years his junior, her wild teenage daughter, and the teen-ager's toddler girl. Verlan supported all of them and was the anchor of this chaotic household, an unconventional middle American home. Touchingly, the little girl took us into her tiny room and told us we could bed down there for the night with her.

After Des Moines and then Council Bluffs, where I imagined the tribes lining up to face each other on the cliffs over the Missouri, we turned straight north and the Great Plains opened out to our left.

On first experience, the plains are unsettling, intimidating-- no doubt here that an individual is insignificant to the universe, that survival is a struggle, and yet, that people are what matter most. Under the open sky with flat land and straight highways going directly north or directly west, the mind will wander into the past, populating that landscape with familial memories. In my mind's eye I saw my grandmother traveling in a covered wagon, and I saw her mother pumping water from the well in snowstorm. I saw houses plunked down on the plain with a 360 degree view and a vast sky dome above all. Until the foothills of the Rockies, this is our America.

Mom and Dad were both from small farms in the southeast portion of the state. We turned left at Sioux City and continued west across the plains. When we saw a sign that indicated Herrick off to the south, Linda dug out her instructions from Mom, who had lived there for a brief time in her youth. Its current population hangs in at 105.

"Okay, here's the address," Linda said, reading Mom's notes. "Roland lives on the north side of the east end of the street."

"WHICH street?" I asked. She repeated the instructions.

We arrived at a crossroads resembling a downtown. I headed east, as this must be "the street," and there, not far, on the north side, was a mailbox with Roland's name and himself standing by the box under an intimidating expanse of nothing but sky. We went into the small house with no paint at all on the exterior. The door opened into the kitchen, where every surface was covered with something, seemingly everything that had ever come into this house: mail, dishes, silverware, storage containers with nothing in them, pots and pans, souvenirs from restaurants and casinos, matchbooks, tools. Every wall was stacked floor to ceiling with neatly-folded newspapers.

"I was proud of your Mom when she won 'volunteer of the year,'" he said, walked to a stack of papers, and extracted the very newspaper containing the story of this award. "Now let's go to dinner, my treat."

Roland got into his pickup and we followed him in the Saab. He took us right back to that crossroads intersection and into a large barn-like building also with no paint. This was the general store, day care, tavern, pool hall, gun shop, game room, laundry, pharmacy, and restaurant.

Along the right was a counter with candy and gum; toward the back was a pot-bellied stove. There was a pool table, a playpen, a folding clothes line, and some round tables at which people were playing cards, and along the left wall some ancient booths with ripped upholstery. "Hey, Roland," came greetings, accompanied by questioning gazes and stares at us. Roland nodded but was otherwise mum.

There was a menu on a plastic board on the wall, and Roland said, "Order anything you want." Our choices consisted of things that might be heated in a microwave—we settled on burritos and burgers, and the bill for four of us was under $10. While we waited for our food, a man came over to the booth, holding his thumbs in the bib of his overalls and eyeing us up and down.

"How's it going, Roland?"

"Fine, just fine," Roland said, nothing more.

You could SEE the ears of the card-players tilt our way. Facing silence, the man returned to the stove, but the entire table of card-players had inched closer to our booth. We smiled at Roland, and our food came. We looked up, and the round table of card-players was about a foot closer to our booth. They were straining to hear our conversation. Curiosity hung palpably in the room, and Roland was playing them masterfully. Roland abruptly rose, approached the card table, and announced in a quiet voice, "These are Leota's girls."

Cards flew into the air, and everyone whooped. My mother had not been in this town for fifty years, but women came over to hug us. Someone said, "We would have recognized you anywhere." Then they went back to their pinochle game, we ate our microwaved dinner, and life went on as usual at the Herrick store.

After South Dakota, it was a straight path back to Oregon. Somehow this journey had furthered my education, me with my fancy Ph.D., and the plains had become the fulcrum of my personal geography. I was connected to the heart of our land more than I had ever realized part of my heritage and my identity.

Rufus Red & Chippy

By Joan (Michalke) Ritchey

The little Rufus hummingbirds
    Came to our feeders one spring day
And all throughout that summer
    This was their place to stay.

Then we were surprised
    When fall and winter came along
The nectar must have pleased them
    They tarried here... not moving on.

About the very same time
    Of the hummers' arrival
I spotted a chipmunk scurrying about
    But, hiding for survival.

'Chippy' made his home
    Underneath our driveway hedge
I'd whisper to him each morning as I
    Fed him walnut halves and bread.

It was a pleasant winter
    So Chippy decided, I guess, to stay
But, I think he enjoyed himself
    While on our place he played.

One day I found a Rufus hummer
    Lying dead upon the deck
He'd flown into the plate glass window
    And broke his little neck.

That afternoon while watering plants
    From the barrel used to gather rain
I found the little chipmunk there
    And was stricken with the pain.

I think Chippy must have hopped
    Onto the bucket rim
Then fell into the water
    And drown from the tiring swim.

I carefully carried Rufus Red & Chippy
    To a special spot
Underneath a rose bush
    In our flower garden plot.

I dug a shallow grave
    And placed them side by side
Their mound was warmly moistened
    By the tears I could no longer hide.

That year, in June, the prettiest roses
    I have ever seen in bloom
Were the large bright flowers
    Where the two friends were entombed.

Mottle-hued, like Chippy's fur
    The rose aromas so wide spread
And the vibrant, brilliant color…
    Iridescent—Rufus red.

His Mistake

By Roger G. Ritchey

From our in-home real estate office I watched the unfamiliar, older, white van pull up to my shop, then slowly back up to turn around. The driver stopped, got out and walked into my always-open three-bay machine shed. He came back a minute later lugging something. Something of mine!

For several weeks during July and August the rural neighborhood west of Forest Grove had been victimized by a half-dozen bold, daylight robberies. A nondescript beat- up white van, with the last three license numbers 919, was the vehicle used by the thief. There was gripping concern in our rural community, because on one occasion the spaced out robber had confronted a young mother, and her home-schooled children with a knife. This 'doper' guy was brazen and vicious!

I went to the closet by our front door and grabbed my ancient over and under shotgun-rifle that I'd inherited from my grandfather. Then I stepped out onto our front porch—the thief had to drive back by to exit our country place.

The driver slowly pulled away from the shop and down our driveway. The van looked like it had spent most of its unhappy automobile life on the Oregon coast, judging by the peeling orange rust. I held up my arm signaling for him to stop and then chambered a shell into the quaint, double-barreled gun. The metallic click was very audible in the still, muggy air!

I raised my arm more forcefully...still no hesitation by the van driver. Then my eye caught the last three numbers of the license plate—919! It was him, and probably thinking we weren't home during the day. Through the open van windows, I saw a flash of metal. Maybe he was armed? He began to accelerate! I took quick aim and put a rifle shot just over the top rear of his vehicle.

Then he really floor-boarded the old Ford Econoline van! A gusty cloud of oily black smoke shot out and the back tires were churning rocks on our graveled driveway.

I levered in another rifle shell and shot into his front tire! There was a metallic ping as the hollow-point bullet hit both metal and rubber. Then a resounding pop! Rapidly changing barrels, I fired the 12-gauge shotgun into the rear of his rusty van shattering one window. The smell of gunpowder was pungent in the still air! I heard his front tire rim clunking on the gravel driveway.

The blocky shaped vehicle started veering to the right, edging closer to my half-acre fishpond.

There is just a scant few feet between our driveway and the pond and a steep bank drops off into the reservoir. The old van began to slowly slip into the deepest water and, with the open or broken windows; it was taking on water like the Titanic.

I heard him scream "Son-of-a-Bitch"...as the van slowly submerged. By damn! It looks like 919's robbing days are over.

I don't believe that I have an ingrained mean streak, but I was kinda hoping he couldn't swim.

A Hitch in Time

By Susan Schmidlin

Rural life isn't all it is cracked up to be. Repairing is a necessity that requires more time and effort than all the actual work on a farm. My farm is filled with fixes.

It takes the whole winter to get all the summer gear back into shape. The summer is usually too busy with real farming for many repairs. All the winter barn cleaning, mud hauling, and road smoothing paraphernalia tends to sit idle during harvests until pressed into action with only hap-hazard patches.

Yet, old farm implements yearn for constant attention to stay in working order. Quick fixes using good old fashioned imagination and inspiration lead to interesting dilemmas. Often we had been able to cobble things up to make due in a pinch, but isn't not a pretty process or a pretty end result for that matter.

This must be the reason most farmers do not loan out any power farming tools. It just takes too long to describe in full detail what repairs had been made and how the borrower needs to deal with the quirks of that renovation.

A simple toggle switch can become a Rube Goldberg - inspired, domino effect, contraption. A hunk of twine becomes a pull cord threaded through an old belt buckle for tension, it in turn tips a fulcrum based teeter totter that hits a bent flat strap, which clears a bit of rust from the starter, allowing for a mini electrical jolt, which finally turns over the engine.

Turning the engine off requires a whole new set of directions completely unconnected to starting the darn thing.

My husband remembers every bit of scrap metal, wood, nut, bolt, bungee cord, and baling twine on the farm. He also is able to use more of those items than any other human when attempting to repair a broken fender, or splintered rake handle, or worn out sprocket. He is the master of temporary solutions that somehow never find themselves completely right again.

We had inherited an old honey wagon from my dad. For those not familiar with this type of equipment, this is a polite term for a manure spreader. The honey wagon is used to get the manure out of the barn and into a field where nature takes its sweet time to process the stinky slop into fertilizer. Dad had even used some temporary/permanent fixes to keep the wagon in working order long before he passed it on to us.

Our newly acquired wagon did not have a good hitch for tractors. It was originally used with an actual horse to supply the horsepower. Although we are not opposed to using equine power, I am more inclined to use more modern methods to quickly dispose of the muck that fills my barns.

Hubby decided to fix the hitch so it would hook up to the tractor easily. Didn't look difficult at all. When he looked closer at his project, he noticed a split in the four foot wooden beam that connected to the front axle. Instead of replacing the beam, he used metal strapping cinched tight in a couple places to keep the crack from growing.

Fearing the beam was still not strong enough, he said he wanted to 'dapt' something onto the structure. I heard other old farmers in the local area refer to this same word. It was not in any dictionary that I have ever come across. Perhaps it is slang for 'adapt,' but I tend to believe that it means slapping a bunch of stuff together for the heck of it.

While I fretted over an uncommon word, he commenced with the strengthening by 'dapting' two boards on each side of the beam and securing them with baling twine. Finally, moving on to the reason a repair was needed in the first place, he looked at the end of the newly decorated tongue. Designed to meet up with a horse harness, it was just too floppy to connect with the solid steel of the tractor hitch. He decided that this issue could be addressed with some old wire wound around the beam and onto the ends of the metal, thereby creating a firm stem.

Once the wire was wrapped tight, a moment was taken for a final inspection. He noticed the boards he secured earlier to the split beam were too loose. Those 'dapted boards' kept sliding around. He grabbed a hunk of broken tree limb and whittled the end to a point. The problem was solved by jamming the limb under the strapping and baling twine where the boards were wiggly. This effectively (or ineffectively) cinched that whole shaft tight.

His repair of the hitch indeed made it stronger and readily attachable to the tractor except for a small problem. He had added about thirty pounds to the already unwieldy aperture. It would require bodybuilder strength to hook it to the tractor. Undaunted, he smiled as he looked over his handiwork and announced that it was almost as good as new. That was saying a lot for an antique honey wagon that had seen a lot of use. It was also not true.

Although I cannot help attach or detach the behemoth hitch, it has held up going on ten years now. This quick little patch up seems to be in for the long haul. I'm not sure if all his other corrections will last as long.

Season after season of temporary fixes that were never made permanent, show like battle scars of a long, hard fight. However, with all the work it has done over the years, that old honey wagon deserves to be a little eccentric. And so it is.

$\mathscr{S}$EEDS OF...

Section V – Reflecting

American Graffiti

By Karen R. Hessen

Ochre, orchid and olive – more colors than a sixty-four pack of Crayola crayons. Freight trains, once the life-blood of American commerce, still course the veins of our nation. Their brilliance stands out against summer's drying crops. Ribbons of color trace the landscape and lace through tunnels across America. The colors of the boxcars blur together as I traverse the collage of states we call the USA at seventy-five miles per hour.

Gray – the color of quandary. Why am I surprised to see them here in America's mid-section? My customary air travel takes me above them and I have forgotten. I am driving across the continent to watch the Yankees play ball in the Twin Cities, to view the majesty of Mt. Rushmore, to wonder at the mystery of Devil's Tower, to pay homage at the Laura Ingalls Wilder museum, to walk with bare feet in the pebbled waters of Lake Superior, to stand reverently on the blood-soaked soil of Little Big Horn's battlegrounds, to watch the buffalo forage on the native grasses of their natural habitat and dine at the Mall of America. These roving galleries of color are not listed in my AAA Tour Book. I don't expect to see them. But, I am glad they amaze my spirit.

Black, brick and brown – the various hues painted upon the rust colored canvases only as high as the arm can reach. Like paint swatches in The Home Depot, one after the other in combinations that both elevate and depress the mood. Vandalism, I suppose, but somehow, lovely, alluring, belonging here.

Tan, teal and tangerine – designed on rectangle shapes that remind me of bolts of fabric in the yardage store. The same designs we wrap our bodies in so we can stand out from the crowds. Each proudly displays a pattern as unique as the snowflakes of winter – appealing to an individual taste. The choices seem unlimited. Some with letters of the alphabet, some with geometric motifs, others an eclectic collage from the artist's imagination. They tease the thought.

Peach, plum, and periwinkle – artwork reminiscent of the kaleidoscope from my childhood – bright changing shapes which erased the boredom caused by long summer hours of unschooled inactivity. Here they break the monotony of miles of sunflower-covered prairie and dry barren grasslands. I welcome their intrusion on the landscape.

Mint, maize and mahogany – like the patches of a giant quilt that is bordered by the Atlantic and the Pacific and our national borders in the North and South – a gigantic moveable feast for the eyes. Today it rides through Oregon, tomorrow Montana, next week Kansas, then Kentucky. Only restricted by the rails it sits on. More offerings than the eye can capture – always changing, always moving, always captivating.

Salmon, shamrock and silver – boxcars more colorful than a Norman Rockwell, more chaotic than an Edward Munch, but art just the same; exquisite, charming pieces of Americana; art that is an image from today's culture. It speaks in the voice of the unemployed, the underemployed, the lonely, the bored and the desolate. It also speaks of unrecognized talent and potential, of dormant energy and untapped imagination. It pictures both hope and despair.

Canary, carnation and copper – move the boxcar art from coast to coast. Let it ride the rails. Display our great promise across the land. Color America with expectation and optimism!

Confetti

by Joan Graves

It was the morning after Barack Obama was reelected President. I had stayed up the night before to watch his acceptance speech. He was like a rock star. When the speech was over the Vice President and both their families came on stage. It reminded me of the end of a Saturday Night Live episode. Then searchlights beamed up from the back of the stage, reminiscent of a rock concert, and tons of confetti were released, which sparkled in the diffuse light.

It was a clear, sunny, but gusty fall morning. I was in my car, at Sunset Esplanade, a strip mall, listening to the sound track for the movie 'To Rome with Love.' The second cut, 'Amanda mia, amore mio,' was playing. It's very lively, with something that sounds like spoons clacking and a thumping bass. A profusion of maple leaves were lit up by the sun and carried aloft by the gusts. The leaves flew like so much confetti.

Autumn Gusts

by Susan K. Field

Ginkgo leaves rain overnight, blanketing earth;

distant winds beckon, in a flurry they're

gone.

"Where are you now golden fans?"

Coyote Moon

by Wafford Tornieri

Moon, moon, dancing brightly over me,
playing shadow. My eyeshine light

she may not notice. Her shadows
are just eyes of rock,

chocolate scratches turning,
metaphors for eye holes.

So space from here curves everything.

The Birds Of November

By Phil Pochurek

By the first of November
Most of the colors have been washed
From the leaves left on the trees
And the rest are on the ground.
Geese are circling overhead
Flying in great sweeping Vee's
In lines across the sky.
Honking their good-bye's
In a dissonant sound,
Familiar to all of us
Who hear them on the ground
That winter's not far behind.
The high winds have come
To help carry them where
There's food and fairer weather.
Where they can eat and rest their wings
Of goose down and tired feather.
It's the last of fall.
Most of the trees are bare
And the fields are plowed for the winter.
When the geese heed the call
And all take to wing,
Filling the skies with their melancholy cries
As the birds of November sing.

Douglas Fir Tree

By Marilyn Schmidlin

I stand tall with strength and courage as I reach
    toward the Son
My roots are growing more stable; then further intertwined
    on this Rock cliff
I have aged gracefully with my family who are deeply
    rooted beside me
My internal growth rings show my endurance,
    wisdom and love
However, Greedy humans have unrespectfully found
    my fortress under false pretense
Dirty hands, in addition to, rotten souls have
    dug, prodded and scared my pillar foundation
Violators have taken firm ground to replace innocence
    with deep stress cracks including infractions
Erosion has teamed up with these deceivers, in which
    time intensifies the strain of forces
I silently look at my past and present while I'm becoming
    more aware of my preceding future
Not as if life is flashing before my eyes, but time
    slowed down: so slow, to a crawl
Inspecting where my footing is now residing plus repairing
    the relationship with my Lord
Thankful God is the mainstay of my Soul and is with me
    wherever I may go
I will stand tall with strength and courage
    as I reach for the Son

pier

By Mary Jane Nordgren

'tween furrowed earth and fluid perpetuity
within the onslaught
of tidal flux
now drowned, now bared to sun

within the onslaught
condemned to rot and death
now drowned, now bared to sun
mussel-bound and barnacled

condemned to rot and death
intersecting stubborn life and loss
mussel-bound and barnacled
jutting into infinity

intersecting stubborn life and loss
of tidal flux
jutting into infinity
'tween furrowed earth and fluid perpetuity

(early version first published in 4 and 20 poetry)

How Like Life

By Alisa J. Hampton

Thick, deep fog
Eerie and impenetrable.
As we drive the familiar,
Everyday route to town,
Nothing is familiar.
Nothing is visible beyond the immediate.
Is this the same world?
The huge cedar we've passed a hundred times
Leaps out
And we startle.
I'm positive the big world is out there,
But tendrils of doubt seep in like the wet, cold air.

How like life, I think.
Some days you can't see beyond
The looming responsibilities,
Or the emergencies at hand.
The rest of the world drops from view.
Some days, maybe that's ok.
Because that's as much as we can handle.
All I can see is the bend ahead
And the squirrel who just darted in front of us.
I turn right at the crossroads –
Heading toward town.
Going on faith that the road continues.
Taking it on faith that the world is still out there…
Even if I can't see it.
Comforted by the belief that,
Someday,
The fog will lift.

In Debt

By Paula Sheller Adams

The good news, the blessing is
we are so deep in debt, inescapable and hopeless.

In debt to love we never earn
In debt to dirt and trees and little sticky leaves
In debt to clouds and rain – to oxygen for breath
In debt for every steaming cup
    sipped at a corner table with a friend
In debt for casseroles brought in at time of need.

In debt to enemies, to pain, to grief
In debt to rocks and thorns and weeds
    and life-creating death
In debt to grass that feeds the grazers,
    to grazers feeding wolves
    and to the fruiting flower--
    helpless without the stinging bee.

The blessing is this permanence of debt,
inexorable, crisscrossing, relieved by
    no payments,
    no IOU's
    no saintly behavior
    no years upon our knees—
this dos-a-dos of life, that wants
a guiltless, glad and open-armed embrace.

And in whatever world may follow this
I want no balanced ledger in that heaven
lest needing nothing of each other, we
should find it hell.

Seeds of... Volume II   CONTRIBUTORS

Paula Sheller Adams is a retired teacher, certified family therapist and former founder of a successful small-town newspaper. In retirement, a particular joy has been leading adults, children, and institutionalized teens in creative writing. This is her poetry's fifth publication appearance.

Lois Akerson, retired teacher and legal secretary, lives in Forest Grove, OR. Her work has been published in Nostalgia Magazine, News Times Newspaper and Seeds of . . . A member of Writers in the Grove, her focus is on family-friendly stories with positive values.

Julie K. Caulfield. I firmly believe our stories need to be told. I have a short story called "Beau" published by Linden Hill in an anthology called "Amazing Cat Tales," and an honorable mention with a Poem called "The Lady in Red" elsewhere.

Susan K. Field lives and writes in Forest Grove. She's a native Oregonian, holds a master's degree in writing and her poetry, fiction and nonfiction have been published in various magazines, journals and books.

Eva Foster currently resides with her husband in Hillsboro, Oregon. Drawing from years of personal journaling, she continues to learn how to put memories and experiences into essays and poetry. A mother of three, and grandmother of six... Life is abundant.

Everett E. Goodwin, poet, essayist and fiction writer, has been a teacher and social worker. His pieces have been published in many periodicals and journals. He is also interested in singing and writing for musicals.

Joan Graves is a Hillsboro, Oregon, writer who has published in TAWK Press, 4 & 20 Poetry, and Rain. She can be reached at foracanthus@gmail.com.

Ross M. Hall, a founder of "Willamette Week," ran business operations at OGI and Sharp Labs of America. He enrolled in creative writing at Clark College upon retirement in 2002. Ross lives in Vancouver, Washington.

Alisa J. Hampton, a multi-linguist, is a composer of choral and handbell music. Since retiring from her position as chairperson of the Forest Grove School Board, she has been accepted as a member of the Bells of the Cascades.

Matthew Hampton is a Freshman at Forest Grove High School and an active member of Children's Educational Theatre in Salem, Oregon, known for his wit and outrageous sense of humor. You can find him volunteering weekly at the Forest Grove City Library.

Sarah K. Hampton, a Junior at Forest Grove High School, is president of the school's Poetry Club and an award-winner in mathematics and science.

Bunny Lynne Hansen is an ordained Christian Minister and retired Pastor of thirty five years. She resides in Banks, Oregon. with Ed, her husband of forty five years, plus a Rat Terrier and a Doberman Pincher.

Karen R. Hessen is a speaker and author of inspirational nonfiction and humor. She frequently contributes to anthologies. Karen writes the columns, "Out of the Ark," and "Zap, Kackle, Plop" for *THE LINCOLN CITY NEWS GUARD*. Contact Karen at *karenwrites@frontier.com*.

Hannah Thuku Kolehmainen lives in Forest Grove with her husband and boys. She is an occupational therapist and does hospice work. She is an avid gardener, cook, educator, and writer.

Animal behaviorist **Rosemary Douglas Lombard** explores turtles' cognitive potential. A winner of prizes in poetry, fiction, and nonfiction, she has just completed a chapbook of poems about turtles and is writing *Diode's Experiment: A Box Turtle Investigates the Human World.* -- *"The Miner in Me"* was published in *Work Literary Magazine, www.workliterarymagazine. com/submission/rosemary-douglas-lombard-3262012/.*

D.K. Lubarsky, retired Physical Therapist and sculptor, DK Lubarsky turned her hand to writing serious poetry, and essays on the lives of 5 older women as they take their senior years head on with a twist of poignancy and humor.

Muriel Marble, recently deceased widow of Pastor Ivan Marble and mother of nine Marbles so inspiring in the Forest Grove community, gave a life as well as writings on compassion and faith.

Sandra Mason is author of *Econolingua, Poems Along the Way,* and *Lost and Found* as well as "Hearing Ophelia," a classic in feminist Shakespearean studies. Founder of the Northwest Poets Concord, she lives in just the right spot by the sea.

Fred Melden, co-director of Conversations With Writers and author of Education Goals and American Values, lives in Hillsboro, Oregon. His writes and publishes one poetry chapbook annually.

At twenty-six, **Mitch Metcalf** was told, "No one as young as you could have done all those things." Now in his sixties, this rockhound, photographer, artist and technology consultant shares some of those stories, sure to take readers to unknown places.

G. A. Meyerink (Gretchen Keefer) comes from a family of writers, although she is the only one who writes short fiction. Her stories are usually family friendly and hopefully inspirational. She plans to write more when she "retires," someday.

Jessica Page Morrell lives in Portland, Oregon, surrounded by writers, and watches the sky in all its moods. She writes with depth, wit and clarity on writing and creativity, contributes to magazines and anthologies, and is the author of five books for writers and *Voices From the Streets*.

Susan Springer Munger, retired academic, has written radio commentary, business articles and a money management handbook. Now writing for pleasure, Susan concentrates on memoir, poetry and fun mysteries, plus stories for and about her children.

Mary Jane Nordgren, author of EARLY: Logging Tales Too Human to be Fiction, is founder of Writers in the Grove and President of TAWK Press. She has recently taken a class in script writing from master teacher/screen writer, Cynthia Whitcomb.

Phil Pochurek has been writing poems for about 45 years... my poet grandfather flows through my pen often and helped me fill up two books: "The Life We Choose" and "The Other Side Of The River." My paint brush is a pen...

Charles E. Pritchard, D.O. "I was born at a very young age." Chuck wrote his essay to honor his beloved wife Betty, who has been with him in the Peace Corps in Fiji, through medical school and setting up pediatrics practice and now retirement. Chuck is an active member of Writers in the Grove.

Nel Rand is the author of two books, Mississippi Flyway, which won a notable book award from Blue Ink Revues, top ten books of the year award from Foreword Book Revues. The Burning Jacket received a Willa finalist award (2011).

Joan (Michalke) Ritchey's first book of poetry, From Him... Through My Fingertips, came out in 2008; narrative fiction, The Brooch, in 2013, and her collection of short stories, Captured Reflections, in 2015. "Tell your story. It is great fun."

Roger G. Ritchey began writing several years ago and now finds he must write stories or try to compose poetry. His down-home style and humor are captured in 2013's Hankering...For the way It Was. Mostly true Stories and Other Lies will be born in 2015.

After success public speaking, **Rebecca Robinson** wrote and shared her stories with other women in life writing classes. She co-presented a workshop at the Northwest Poets Concord in 2012 and facilitated the Hillsboro writers' group Parallel Play for three years.

Marilyn Schmidlin, multifaceted young businesswoman, loves orchids and nurtures a number of exotic varieties for friends as well as at home on the family farm. Marilyn writes of her love of Nature and of her faith.

For many years, **Susan Schmidlin** worked outside the home, but now she is full-time on the family farm near Vernonia. She writes with wit and compassion about rural rocks and hills, and people.

Gerlinde Schrader has enjoyed writing poetry and short-stories for about seven years. She has self-published four volumes in her specialty, children's stories. A great-grandmother, she has lived in Hillsboro since retiring from OHSU Dental School.

A retired policeman, **Joe Schrader's** poetry has appeared in The North Plains Beacon, The Tualatin Times, The Central Oregon Senior Times, and the Golden Years News. He has self-published The Toadstool Chronicles and Joe's Poems, in which "I Shot an Arrow" and "The Squirrels Speak to Me" have previously been published.

Barbara Schultz, Spiritual Advisor, Writer, Gardener, Lover of life, and a late bloomer. She moved to the US when she was already 50, graduated with a BAC aged 57, and started writing seriously when almost 70.

William L. Stafford attended schools in Forest Grove and Oregon State University. He has worked in seven different industries, including twenty years running the family slaughter house and doing foreign consulting work. "I wrote during all those years, but always for myself. I still live on the farm where I was born."

Mark Thalman is the author of Catching the Limit, Fairweather Books (2009). He received his MFA from the University of Oregon, and has been teaching in the public schools for 33 years. Thalman is the editor of poetry.us.com. For more information please visit *www.markthalman.com*.

Wafford Tornieri works at the Chelonian Connection lab, where he studies coldblooded cognition. He writes by tapping on a communication board. He likes to dance and to imagine delightful days in the mountains. Then he examines the home flowers. "Coyote Moon" is Wafford's first publication.

B. R. Walker . Travels and multitudes of people have inspired three books of genealogy, poetry, a play and several published articles. Most recently, "Tribute to a Mail Carrier" in Forest Grove News Times, Dec, 2014, and a book of drawings, "Scribbling Forest Grove."